The Meditators

The Meditators

by

DOUGLAS SHAH

LOGOS INTERNATIONAL
Plainfield, New Jersey

GOOD READING LIMITED
London, England

Biblical quotations used in the text of this book are noted as follows: KJV, the King James Version of 1611; NEB, the New English Bible, © copyright 1961, 1970 by the delegates of Oxford University Press and the syndics of the Cambridge University Press; NASB, the New American Standard Bible, © copyright 1960, 1962, 1971, 1973, by the Lockman Foundation.

Further acknowledgments: Much of the material on pp. 30–33 was drawn from "The Power of Positive Non-Thinking," (*Newsweek*, January 7, 1974) which is copyright 1974 by Newsweek, Inc., all rights reserved, and is used by permission; extensive quotations from "The Alpha State Lets the Mind Take Wings," by Diane Shah (*The National Observer*, August 23, 1971) appear on pp. 105 f. and are used by permission; a quotation from p. 11 of *The Latent Power of the Soul* by Watchman Nee, copyright © 1972 by Christian Fellowship Publishers, New York, all rights reserved, appears on p. 111 and is used by permission. The author also wishes to acknowledge his reliance upon *The Religions of Man* by Huston Smith (pp. 80–82, 125, 129–130, 195, 200, 159–160, 163, 175–176) copyright © 1958 by Huston Smith and used by permission of Harper & Row, Publishers, Inc. for some of the material in chapter seven of this book.

THE MEDITATORS

International Standard Book Numbers: 0–88270–125–8 (hardcover)
0–88270–126–6 (softcover)
Library of Congress Catalog Card Number: 75-7478
Logos International, Plainfield, New Jersey 07061

To my wife, Sue.
Also, to the searching masses of our human family—
in hopes that they will find "the truth."

Contents

Introduction

Adam strolled through the Garden of Eden with God. They talked and laughed and enjoyed each other immensely. It was a beautiful relationship. Yet, as wonderful as it was, there was an aspect of this communion that kept Adam from being perfectly happy. He not only wanted to walk and talk with God, he also wanted to be like God. He wanted to be one with God.

That same hunger lingers to this day in the hearts of men and women all over the world. And one of the means many of them have used to try to satisfy that desire has been meditation.

Now, in these last days of the twentieth century, meditation has had a fantastic revival. People from every walk of life are embracing the different beliefs that are founded on meditation, like Rosicrucianism, Bahai, Hare Krishna, Scientology, Hinduism, Buddhism, Confucianism, and many more. These are sincere people who are so devoted to their beliefs that their presence and works have become known to millions.

Yet, there is something missing. An ingredient that makes even their most strenuous efforts go unrewarded. For there isn't enough in any of us to enable us to reach beyond the stars. The peace that truly fills every particle of our being eludes us all in the most mysterious way. Why is that?

The author of this book has a startling answer to that question. Now let him open some doors that have been closed to many of us. Let knowledge, not ignorance, hold sway.

MICHAEL ESSES, D.H.L.

The Meditators

CHAPTER I

East Rises in the West

The Searching Heart

Sita Ram, oh Sita Ram . . . A new day was dawning. Within minutes, the religious shrine, nestled in a forest of trees, was silhouetted against the eastern sky. The sound of birds and the clang of heavy bells around the necks of sacred cows mingled with the chanting of worshippers that lifted on the early morning air and echoed through the forest. *Sita Ram, oh, Sita Ram* . . .

Lying on the grass beneath a large Pepal tree, was a man in a saffron robe—my Yogi grandfather, Ishwar Dayal. He was there as a fulfillment of prophecy.

Ishwar Dayal was born in 1868 in Laheria Sarai, North Behar, India, into a Hindu household. His father died at an early age, and he found himself as part of a large joint family household—a common Hindu social custom, according to which several interrelated families live together in the same house.

Ishwar Dayal was married at the young age of twenty to Anughra (meaning "Grace"), which was rather unusual according to general Hindu social patterns. After a year of marriage a son was born to them, who died shortly after birth. But after another year, another son was born, strong

1

and healthy—an auspicious occasion, for Hindu families look upon the birth of a son as an expression of God's special favor.

However, the sense of pride and joy mellowed when the horoscope of the boy was read. It revealed that the boy's father would "leave his home forever and become unknown to his people." Already spiritually inclined, with a deep yearning to seek "something better," shortly after the birth of his son he left his home and family on a Yogi's quest for truth. Above all, he desired to be "united" and "linked" with God. And so, here he was.

As he awoke, the early morning sights and sounds seemed to inspire him to renew his quest for yet another day. This was only the beginning of what would be an exhaustive, six-year search of all that the religions of India had to offer. Did he really know what he was searching for? Perhaps not, but he felt that he would recognize the "truth" when he found it.

Barefooted, and attired in a one-piece saffron-colored cloth wrapped around his waist with one of its loose ends over his shoulder, he was determined, as part of his spiritual quest, to deprive himself of all human comforts, and so he existed on a diet of roots and fruit.

Did he have to be out there, wandering, searching?

Yes. He had not found "truth" and enlightenment in education. An accomplished scholar, he had studied and become fluent in Sanskrit and well-versed in the Hindu scriptures—Gita, Vedas, Mahabharat, and Ramayana. But he had not found his answer in the realms of the intellect.

He had both position and wealth. As a tax collector for the Maharajah of Darbhanga in Behar, India, he received a munificent stipend. Besides which, he was of the *Kayastha* caste of Hindu society, which consisted of the intelligentsia and were basically involved in administrative functions, ranking second only to the *Brahmins* who were priests and monks.

Grandfather did a lot of what he called "sitting." With crossed legs and closed eyes, he spent hours each day musing on God and on nature—seeking for some central "truth" which could give his entire life a sense of coherence and unity. But the sitting seldom satisfied the longing, and to alleviate the frustration of searching and not finding, Ishwar Dayal became voluntarily addicted to *Ganja*, a narcotic not unlike marijuana.

Here, at last, he was able to attain the spiritual "highs" he wanted to experience by expanding his consciousness. But they lasted only as long as the effects of the drug. It was not what he had committed his life to finding.

And so he went into the Himalayan foothills, to chant to, and meditate upon the gods and goddesses of Hindu religious heritage. In the rain, in the cold, in the sun, the Yogi spirit ruled supreme—never wavering from the path, pressing on with persistence to find the "truth" through spiritual transcendence and meditation.

Deliberating and contemplating with religious mystics, gurus, and priests, he spent months in temples, religious shrines, and centers of spiritual pilgrimage. The smell of fresh flower petals, dimly lit prayer rooms, smooth tile floors, and richly-adorned idols became as familiar to him as the family surroundings of an earlier age.

My grandfather died in 1964. As it happens, he found what he was looking for, and before this book is over, we will see what it is he found, and how. To me, he stands as a giant, even among that unique class of Yogis, who spend all their lives seeking, and are considered the masters of the search. He started out knowing nothing, save a feeling deep in his heart that there had to be something better. That same Eastern spirit of searching has invaded literally millions of hearts in the Western world today.

Searching on the Western Front

The Himalaya Mountains and the Indo-Gangetic plains of India form a haven and nesting ground for the ardent meditator. But the spirit of meditation is not restricted by geographical boundaries; it pervades every level of human existence. Every human being, whether inclined to be a participator or a spectator, becomes at some point in his life—a meditator.

Dawn comes to a shopping center in a typical American suburb. The day begins, not with chants and cow bells, but with the "chainy" clanging of grocery carts, and the bell of a cash register as it completes a total.

In the aisles of the supermarket, busy Americans push loaded grocery carts and pull insistent children away from the candy shelves. Brows furrow and heads shake at the rapidly rising prices interspersed with an occasional smile at the discovery of a sale on a favorite lunchmeat. There's a sigh of relief when it's all done; the total has been tallied and paid for, the groceries are bagged and ready to take to the car.

The way to the clear glass door exit is studded with colorful posters almost crying out for attention. There's the high school dance, the symphony concert, the Blood Donors' Drive, and the classes on Transcendental Meditation. Many pass by, paying no attention, or like myself, throwing no more than a quick, casual glance. I was already outside, when suddenly it struck me: what was that I saw? Deciding on a rerun, I waited till the next person

4

came out, then slipped back in the still-open door, and stood frozen in my tracks in front of the fourth poster.

A few minutes earlier I had been going through a normal act, but now I found myself in a state of heightened mental and spiritual awareness. There, in my neighborhood supermarket, a social and spiritual meta-morphosis far beyond the scope of my wildest dreams had begun, as I gazed at the picture of a "holy man" of India, with flowing beard and smiling face, offering to the West an education in the age-old art of meditation.

Literally millions in America and around the world each day are being confronted with the powerful new medita-tion technique as the solution to the ills of a global generation that is moving at an unprecedented and bewildering pace. With the exception of the zeal dis-played by Christians down the centuries and some Com-munists in recent years, never before has the world been influenced by such a pervasive appeal. Store windows, university campus billboards, and many other public places have been studded with a new message—which in its essence is simply this: "Just learn to meditate. We can teach you. It is not a religion; it is a science. It will make you both calm and energetic. It will revolutionize your entire life."

Evidently, the message has reached and converted many open, pliable hearts and minds—people who were ready for a switch. They had tasted of Western religion, or what passed for it, had failed to find meaning in it, and were left with an unquenchable spiritual thirst.

A "New" Concept?

The art of meditation has been cradled and nurtured in the non-Western countries, yet now America and Europe find themselves with arms and doors open to embrace the mystical Eastern religions and philosophies. The phenomenal increase in travel, cultural exchanges, trade and commerce, and the desire for an international brotherhood of nations has opened up many new channels of communication. Tourism has been an eyeopener. The streets of Calcutta, in India, are not overrun by lions and elephants, and the flashy and grandiose modernization of a place like Tokyo, Japan, is comparable with many of the finest cities in the Western world.

In recent years there has been a religious and philosophical metamorphosis in both the East and the West. According to statistics on the religious belief of our world populace, a little more than a third claim to be adherents of Christianity. Another third of the world marches under the hammer and sickle and lives in Communist countries. Since they practice suppression of religious belief and freedom, there obviously would be some professing religionists in the Communist ranks—more than we probably imagine. We know of more than half a million Jews and Christians in Russia, and reports persist of an underground Christian movement in Red China. The final third of the world's religions is comprised of those who are Hindus, Buddhists, Moslems, Jews, or of some other faith.

Two major spiritual trends of unusual force and depth have emerged in the past two decades. The first is known as the Charismatic Movement, an enthusiastic evangelical Christian movement of the pentecostal variety which embraces a following from every conceivable walk of life and social level, to say nothing of religious background—former Jews, hippies, atheists, Catholics, and Protestants of all denominations, who claim to have found a "new life" in a living Jesus Christ. The Charismatic Movement is receiving increasing attention in the world's media, and its adherents are reported to run well into the millions.

The other movement, though much smaller, is extremely aggressive and is making some fantastic claims and offers of peace, joy, and new energy: meditation, in its deepest or transcendental variety. This particular school of meditation is a movement totally different from the Charismatic Movement. Founded by the inspiration and motivation of Maharishi Mahesh Yogi of India (also the founder of the Spiritual Regeneration Movement), it claims "more than a million people practicing Transcendental Meditation in the world today, about half of whom are Americans," according to one TM instructor.

Human history runs in cycles of actions and reactions. The spiritual pendulum rebelling against all forms of spiritual and religious beliefs, which in the twentieth century had swung so far towards agnosticism and scientific determinism, now seems to be rapidly returning. A new sense of awakening, concerning spiritual fulfillment, is in the process of a meteoric rise all over the world. The human gods of sex, materialism, intellect, and ego provide a temporary form of pleasure, but more than ever people are yearning to find meaning in something spiritual and higher than themselves.

As recently as two decades ago, many Christians from the West that I communicated with considered the missionaries sent out to Eastern countries as "ministers to heathen lands." It is not accurate to say that now the tables seem to have turned, but unquestionably there has been a remarkable response in the West to missionaries from the East. It is not at all uncommon to find in the major cities of America, Buddhist Temples, Vedantas (Krishna Consciousness Centers), Mosques, Zen and Transcendental Meditation Centers, and Yoga schools.

Evangelists from the East

My brother, Ron, visiting from India, was on a flight from New York to Houston, when aboard the plane he was encountered by a group of saffron-robed, shaved-headed, cymbal-clashing Hare Krishna enthusiasts. My brother remained silent, but there was another gentleman from India in the airplane and he was very vociferous about the fact that he had tried it, and that he saw no reason why anyone should be so enthusiastic about it. But the Annual Hare Krishna Jagganath Cart Festival and Parade, observed by the San Francisco Temple of the International Society for Krishna Consciousness, celebrating events in the life of Krishna—a chief god in Hindu mythology, features a Krishna feast, dancing, chanting, and an Indian market, and attracts an ever-growing crowd of spectators. And today, practically every major city in the country has its own street-corner band of chanting krishnas.

The two Eastern religious movements that are probably the most evangelistic in approach and fervent about possessing the spiritual goods to meet mankind's spiritual needs are the two rooted in Hinduism—the Society for Krishna Consciousness (the Hare Krishna worshippers) and the International Meditation Society. These missionaries from the East to the West are by no means a source of financial aid, like the missionaries from the West to the East were. To those in affluent America and the West who have silver and gold, they claim to offer something of yet greater significance.

By far the most sensational of the Eastern missionaries is the self-proclaimed Messiah, Guru Maharaj Ji, from India, founder of the Divine Light Mission. His worshippers adore him as "the one and only perfect Master of this age—the Christ." This plump teen-ager seems to have had his critics. One TV commentator described this leader to a reputed six million followers as a "bag of bogus baloney." *Time* magazine, in its "people" section, June 3, 1974, reported the following concerning his wedding—"His marriage may have been planned in heaven, but sixteen-year-old Guru Maharaj Ji needed earthly approval from Colorado's juvenile court last week before wedding his secretary, Marilyn Lois Johnson, 24." The claims of Guru Maharaj are impressive; however, there is no report of any impressive results in the lives of individuals, except that he does require his followers to be "neat and clean."

But for all such excesses, it appears that the East does have something to say to the West. One-time "sleepy" India, with the revelry of Maharajahs and British Lords, has given birth to a variety of meditation that has suddenly begun to emerge as a significant kind of life-style —highly recommended by its adherents and sweeping over countless thousands of eager Western meditators with each passing month.

I decided that it was time I checked out Transcendental Meditation, and I was in a rather unique position to do so.

An East Indian Perspective

Born in Delhi, India, in 1946, into an upper middle-class family with Hindi as my native language, for the first twenty-two years of my life I was reared in the birthplace of two of the world's major religions—Hinduism and Buddhism. I saw it all, studied it all, talked it all; but it was not until after a period of investigation that I had to affirm what religious beliefs I would personally like to adhere to.

My name, Douglas Shaw, is a westernized version of an East Indian name, and in fact, "Shaw" and "Shah" are used interchangeably in India. My middle name "Maha-boob" means "beloved" in Hindi and other Indian languages. After completing a Bachelor of Arts degree from the University of Calcutta, India, I came to America in 1968 to earn a further degree in Religion and Philosophy at Northwest College in Kirkland, Washington. Being the grandson of the former Yogi and meditator, Ishwar Dayal, I had more than a passing interest in the rise of Transcendental Meditation in America in the 1970's, and decided to investigate thoroughly.

Many people in America fail to understand what meditation really is, and at this point we will define it in general terms: meditation is not just relaxation—though relaxation of your whole being is a part of it. Meditation is not just alertness—though mental and spiritual alertness is an important part of it. Simply stated, it involves achieving a state of "restful alertness." Deep, transcendental meditation is more than just concentration, which is rigid; it is contemplation—a probing of the depths of the mind.

CHAPTER II

Face to Face with the Western Brand

Lecture No. 1

It was certainly packaged differently. Through reading and personal experience, I had tasted of the East Indian version of meditation, but here I found myself in the conference room of a Savings & Loan office in a California city. No flowing Ganges or Himalayan beauty, thronging pilgrims or Rishikesh Ashram (the place where the Beatles received instruction in Transcendental Meditation from the Maharishi personally) filled with the aroma of incense and fresh flower petals. Thickly carpeted with a scattering of comfortable conference chairs around the room, one did feel the touch of semi-sophistication.

Was I alone? By no means. This was a no-cost, no-obligation introductory lecture, and three others besides myself had been sufficiently impressed by the supermarket poster to come and check it out. Like the instructor, they were from the mainstream of middle-class American society—a far cry from the ardent, robed, barefooted, with dot on forehead "lay Sadhus" of India.

Nor was our guru (teacher) a bearded, beady-eyed

11

individual with painted face, matted hair encompassed by brown necklaces, and semi-clothed like an Indian Sadhu (holy man or hermit), but rather a clean-cut, all-American young man in his late twenties. In fact, he mentioned the fact that by day he was employed by a telephone company in the area. Wearing a corduroy coat, wide tie, tinted glasses and a bashful grin, he welcomed all prospective meditators, including myself, in a quiet, reserved manner.

"I must confess that I'm a little disappointed," he began, "that with our newspaper feature story and other advertising, we did not have a better turnout than this. But in any event I have a unique story to tell about Transcendental Meditation because it has given me calmness, super-energy and coordination." He paused and looked over at me. "You must excuse me. I'm a little disjointed today for some reason.

"Instruction in the practice of Transcendental Meditation, as propagated by the Maharishi, involves seven different steps. The first two are lectures, the third stage is the interview with your instructor, and the other four are practical involvement in developing the art of meditating itself. This mental technique should be exercised twice a day, for a period of twenty minutes each time."

"How much does it cost?" I asked.

"The cost of the lessons are presently the following: $200.00 for couples, $125.00 for adults, $65.00 for college students, $55.00 for senior high school students, and $35.00 for junior high school students."

Transcendental Meditation lessons, we were informed, are made available to the public through SIMS (Students International Meditation Society) and IMS (International Meditation Society). Whereas TM is the practical out-working of the Maharishi's program, SCI (Science of

Creative Intelligence) constitutes the theory. The approach is five-pronged: business and industry, students, adults, government agencies, and spiritual.

TM is a mental technique, which anyone can learn; in fact, it is very natural for the human system to come into a state of "restful alertness," for everything in life progresses to a state of fulfillment.

"Don't you think that is a very subjective view?" I asked. "How can you say that everything is progressing to a state of fulfillment?"

"Well, TM offers you this dimension of living," replied the instructor. "You can experience growth effortlessly in every area of your life."

With the aid of a collection of fifteen colorful diagrams on stand-up charts, the instructor proceeded to attempt to support his case factually. "TM will improve your energy, intelligence, and memory recall. It will rid you of stress, which is the deeper aspect of fatigue. In looking at these charts, we see here how, with five to six hours of sleep, the metabolic rate drops eight percent. But, in TM, within three to five minutes the metabolic rate drops sixteen percent. So you see, it is a deeper state of restfulness."

"I don't understand how that happens," exclaimed a young college coed.

"This is due to the alpha, delta and theta waves, all present simultaneously. 'Alpha' waves denote restfulness and delta and theta waves denote alertness."

"Is it not true that bio-feedback can achieve the same sort of effects?" asked another male student.

"I really do not want to discuss the bio-feedback method here today," said the instructor. "We believe TM is the best. In bio-feedback, the mind is flooded only with alpha waves. In TM, only the alpha waves can be detected, but there is also the presence of delta and some theta waves—denoting a simultaneous state of restfulness and alertness.

"TM will permanently establish one in a field of pure intelligence, improve the individual person and contribute to the establishing of world peace. Most TM teachers consider the claim of 'world peace' a little 'corny,' but I am going to mention it anyway. I should clarify the fact that TM is not a religion or philosophy, but a mental technique."

I could see how appealing this sounded to the Westerner who, rightfully or wrongfully, was turned off against established religions or "the Church." But I decided to question the instructor further. "But don't you think it is rooted in, and stems from, the Hindu religion?"

"We'll answer your question in the next lecture," concluded the instructor.

"In closing," he added, "I would like to make you aware of our policy of encouraging prospective meditators to abstain from drugs prior to the practical lessons, in order to maintain a pure nervous system."

Lecture No. 2

The second lecture was similar to the first in some respects, designed to take one into a deeper study of Transcendental Meditation. It began in the same setting, with the same group attending. "TM is not concentration. It is contemplation. Concentration is rigid; contemplation is free to probe the depths of one's mind."

"When are you going to explain the 'mantra' to us?" piped up one searching fellow student, named Joanne.

"A 'mantra' is a word with no meaning. Its sound is a

fluid medium of transcending. TM comes from the Vedic traditions, and that's where we get the mantra from." At this point our instructor, like most TM instructors, refused to discuss the Vedas as "Hindu Scriptures," and the Maharishi's religious ties. Rather, he dismissed it by saying, "We are talking about Indian history, and in India their interpretation of history is different from ours."

"I'm already meditating on my own, without a 'mantra,' " said Joanne.

"You're just not meditating right," said the instructor, a trifle impatiently. "You are without a mantra. You have not been taught systematically. Only an instructor can give you the right mantra." And he sought to compose himself.

"The last recorded revival of Transcendental Meditation is dated at about 5,000 years ago, under the leadership of Shankara. Shankara died at the early age of thirty-three, but was able, prior to his death, to establish the Shankaracharya Seat of Knowledge. This Seat of Knowledge was vacant for 150 years before Guru Dev took on this responsible position."

"Who was Guru Dev?" inquired a male student in the class.

"Guru Dev is the Maharishi Mahesh Yogi's departed master. The Maharishi has been his disciple. In 1958 the Maharishi founded the Spiritual Regeneration Movement. This was not accepted too well by the world, possibly because of its religious connotations. After spending two years in seclusion, the Maharishi in 1961 started his Transcendental Meditation classes with forty students in U.C.L.A. He firmly believes that we are using only six percent of our potential. Transcendental Meditation can help us to utilize one hundred percent of our true potential."

The Plunge

If, after the first two introductory lectures on Transcendental Meditation, you are still determined to meditate Maharishi-style, here is your course of action: after an interview with the instructor and the payment of an initiation fee (Step No. 3), the next four steps take place at a TM Center and will get you involved in what it is really all about.

To the initiation ceremony, you are asked to bring an offering of six flowers, three pieces of fresh fruit, and a white handkerchief. These are placed on an altar before a picture of Guru Dev, the Maharishi's departed master. "Guru Dev" means "Divine leader." In a small room illuminated by candlelight and permeated by incense, you are asked to stand before this altar. The teacher then sings a song of thanksgiving and praise to the entire line of departed Hindu masters who have passed down the knowledge of the mantras.

At the conclusion of the song, the teacher indicates to you that you should continue to kneel silently. Kneeling with you, the teacher begins to repeat the mantra selected for the person. As already stated, the mantra is a fluid, pleasant-sounding, apparently meaningless sound, taken from the Vedas. In Hindu religious tradition it has been used to invoke various Hindu deities, so while it may seem meaningless to an American, it has definite meaning within the Hindu context. In the Hindu religion there are millions of gods, both good and bad, and any of these may possibly be invoked with the appropriate mantra.

The mantra is repeated by the teacher until you can pronounce it rightly. You are then seated for more instruction. If you are like some, you may object to this religious aspect, but most people go along with it in order to learn the technique. For once you have experienced the pleasant sensation of meditating, you may quickly forget any objections to the religious nature of the ceremony and rapidly embrace all that TM has to offer.

After the initiation, three more group lectures are given, and a monthly checking service is provided for meditators. If you are the kind of person who objects to any form of idol worship, Hindu ritual, limited spiritual experience, or expenditure of a fair amount of time and money—you may not be a candidate for TM.

You are on your own now. Aside from the monthly checking service to be sure you are doing it right, you have become a Transcendental Meditator in your own right. From now on, twice each day, for twenty-minute periods, you must sit silently and repeat your "om," "rama," or some other mantra assigned to you by your instructor. As the mantra floats softly through your mind, thoughts will emerge and dissipate like tiny bubbles of psychological stress. "If you really do it right," according to the opinion of most TM instructors, "the sound of the mantra and your thoughts will eventually cease. You will then experience that transcending awareness that, in its pure form, will mean creative energy and intelligence for you." As you continue to do so, the glamorous promises of Transcendental Meditation are supposed to come to pass in your life—intelligence, insight, objectivity, and personal experience will establish the truth or falsehood of some of these seemingly marvelous claims. But whether or not TM passes your acid test, one thing is undeniable: its promises have a tantalizing glamor and appeal if you are searching.*

* The author is indebted to Vail Hamilton, a former TM instructor, for supplying the details of much of the foregoing material on initiation

A Ready and Waiting Audience

World plans for the propagation of TM have been aimed at establishing one center for every one million people. In June, 1974, there were about 7,500 teachers, of which 5,000 live in the United States. There are centers in every country except Russia and China. These two countries are still reviewing the situation.

The Western world, and the United States in particular, seems to be a fertile field for Transcendental Meditation. The meditators—more than half a million of them—flow out from more than 200 World Plan centers in the United States, offering courses in the Science of Creative Intelligence and Transcendental Meditation. It is not like a local club in your neighborhood; it is a mass movement. Do you know what it's really all about?

---

rites. Her description of them has already appeared in "Transcendental Meditation Wants You," by David Haddon (*Eternity*, Nov., 1974).

CHAPTER III

The Great Sweep

How Did It All Begin?

Some Westerners are of the opinion that it all started with the Beatles. It had been around long before the Beatles struck their first electric chord, but what they did do was catapult the concept of transcendental deep meditation into the Western orbit—and many began to receive it gladly. Some felt that the Beatles, in a desperate effort to get off drugs, were willing to yield and turn on to meditation. Whatever their reasons, for millions of Beatle fans, Transcendental Meditation began to take on the appearance of a captivating mystical "trip" at least worth trying.

The concept of transcendentalism is probably as old as the Himalaya Mountains themselves. Man has always sought to transcend in mind and spirit the plane of material and sensuous living. The scriptures of Christianity, Hinduism, Buddhism, Islam, and Judaism all have references to transcendental-type experiences. In fact, the prophet Isaiah in the Old Testament says that waiting in prayerful meditation "before the Lord" will cause one to "mount up with wings" like an eagle.

Transcendentalism—"All American"?

Transcendentalism as a philosophical theory projects the possibility of realities that exist beyond the receptivity range of both the senses and understanding. Through a transcending experience, however, they may be tracked down by the mind intuitively. The analogy of television clarifies this proposition. The air is filled with both sights and sounds transmitted by TV stations. It is only with the use of an antenna and a TV set that we can bring these into a communicable focus by tuning in to a channel of our choice.

In American history, transcendentalism has expressed itself through poetry, speeches, essays, and sermons, and has been commonly accepted as a philosophical and cultural movement that thrived in New England during the nineteenth century. A Transcendental Club led by Ralph Waldo Emerson (1803–1882) included men such as Henry David Thoreau, Frederic Henry Hedge, George Ripley, and Amos Bronson Alcott. The literary influence of these men lingers on, passed on by one generation of Americans to another.

In 1893, an Eastern star appeared in the firmament of Western religions and spiritual thought in the form of Narendranath Datta Vivekananda (1863–1902). Vivekananda was the religious pioneer and leader who founded the Ramakrishna mission and the Vedanta movement. Having experienced a "oneness" with the Hindu godhead, Ramakrishna, he set out to serve mankind. He strongly felt that India could benefit immensely by Western technological methods, which could help alleviate some of its backwardness and extreme poverty. At the same time, America and the West could utilize Indian spiritual insights "to temper some of its overpowering materialistic tendencies."

At the World Parliament of Religions in Chicago in 1893, Vivekananda was the spokesman for Hinduism. Emphatically and enthusiastically, he propagated a gospel that included the concepts of the oneness of existence, the divinity of the soul, and the harmony of religions. Whatever Vivekananda was able to accomplish in the West on a long-term basis is not really the main issue; one thing he did do for sure: he planted the seeds of Eastern religious thought in a fertile Western field.

Measuring Religious Temperature

Literally millions of spiritually-awakened Americans fall into one of two schools of religious thought. The first group holds that all religions are essentially the same, because they lead to the same God. Others accept the more liberal concept that it does not matter what you believe. Each one may do his or her "thing," as long as they are sincere. In reviewing thousands of cases, I find the quality of sincerity is evaluated by many by the extent of one's harmony with God and nature and man. As long as you are not destroying your neighbor's property, not polluting your town, providing for others through charity, and cherishing your own system of religious beliefs, you are an "ok" person.

We cannot deny there are strands of moral and ethical thought that are common to all religions, and some religions do seem to run parallel to each other on many points. In fact, religion itself is the expression of a deep intuition in most humans—that there is a super-power above and beyond us all.

21

But if all religions were indeed the same, we would be a lot closer to world unity than we are today. To see how they differ, take the major world religions which you are familiar with and note their (1) starting point; (2) their end or goal; (3) their answers to human dilemmas and problems; and (4) their lasting influence on mankind, if any. Right away you will realize how different they all really are.

Americans who believe that each one may do his or her own thing, and that sincerity is the only criterion, are not really as religious as they appear. The liberal attitude is commendable, but there are countless numbers of people who deeply believe in things that are destroying them. Adherents to this system of thought are children of the Age of Reason; they declare "the essence of life is what I can see in a test tube and be sure of." To them, the rest is a matter of subjective personal choice and interpretation.

The "reasoning" and "proving" syndrome has permeated into the depths of every sphere of life including religious thought. Many Americans, who find that they cannot prove all they believe as so-called "Christians" about the Bible and God and the hereafter, have rejected their religious heritage. And for many this is only their surface reason for rejection. On talking to hundreds of Americans who at some point rejected their Christian heritage and system of beliefs, it is generally found that such persons are disillusioned not with the truth of the Bible or with Jesus Christ, but rather with inferior Christians and "church systems." Instead of age-old tradition and ritualistic forms, they were looking for a relevant gospel and dynamic action.

It was at this point in the late 1950's and the 1960's in America's religious history that church and Sunday school attendance began to decline in a number of the major denominations. Some of those zealous, evangelistic-type Christians, who just a few years earlier had talked about "reaching the heathen in foreign lands with the Christian message" realized that Christian America was in a state of "spiritual fumbling."

The "Groovy" Contribution

In the meantime, the well-known "hippie" movement, and the drug culture, all intertwined in one, captivated the imagination of millions of American youth. Teen-agers from affluent families turned to search for meaning in hitch-hiking to nowhere, and drugs for "groovy" trips. The social norms and mores of yesterday were shaken at their very roots in an unprecedented fashion.

The upheaval in the structure of the American home and family life did not take place overnight. Parental permissiveness and the educational system have fostered and nourished the youth rebellion movement to its present state. The children of today are the citizens of tomorrow. If they were bred on liberal educational ideals with excessive abuses of freedom and taught to question every tradition and principle, the results were bound to follow, and they did. Never before has the American home been so fragmented, the individual felt so uninhibited to do "his own thing," or society been plagued with myriads of problems of a moral and spiritual nature. We are only reaping now what we sowed earlier.

"Hectic" Does It

The frenetic pace of the affluent American life style has overwhelmed the individual to the point that people are

looking for escape valves and releases. Fancy cars, profes-
sionally decorated houses, social cliques, easily available
charge cards, fashionable vacations, and free love have
their charm still, but they have been around for awhile and
have lost their novelty. Something non-material and a
little "way out" would add some flavor to life—maybe
something like "meditation."

The advertising machine has played it up to the point
that we have begun to believe it really may be worth far
more to you and your society than the money you may pay
to take the basic instruction in it. The pace of life will
finally get a break for at least a few minutes at the start
and finish of each day. It has also promised more
energy—so you can maintain your hectic pace of living.
Sticking to it religiously will at least guarantee you some
period of time each day to just relax. And we Americans
who work hard even at having fun could use a little
relaxation.

Then, too, the *era of openness* is here. One of the most
socially beneficial trends is that of acceptance. I'm a firm
believer in acceptance. Imagine the result if every human
being would accept the other as he is, with respect, even if
there is no total agreement! Converting a person to your
viewpoint, philosophy, or religion is transgressing his will
by force. Spiritual conversion usually takes place where
there is a voluntary yielding of an individual's will to the
higher power that he has committed his life to. This
power—in the realm of some religions, God; in Christianity, Jesus Christ, and so on—is responsible to do the
converting if there is any. Our business is to share with
conviction what we believe. If we cannot do so with
conviction, then quite possibly we're ready for a change.

The world today is open and receptive to just about

anything that can be presented with conviction, and the fascination, mysticism, and charm of Eastern religions and Transcendental Meditation has a powerful impact upon the person who has not yet found a life cause or philosophical niche—a strong, superhuman (divine) peg on which he can hang the hat of his existence in this world.

The trend of religious disillusionment in our time is like an awesome waterfall. Vast multitudes of people who have rejected the form and ritual of their parents' religious organizations, as well as the hypocrisy of so-called "believers," are ready for a switch.

But there are hypocrites in TM, just as there are the genuine meditators, and just as there are true Christians in every church or denomination. There are those who are on the TM bandwagon for another "kick," and some of those who were on a "trip" are now ex-meditators. One young man whom I met in Berkeley told me he had quit meditation for drugs, because it had not given him the trip as fast and as effectively. At the time we had talked, he had quit both and felt liberated in and by Jesus Christ.

Occasionally I meet somebody who tells me I "used to be into TM," speaking of it in the same manner as marijuana or amphetamines, and undeniably the drug scene has contributed to the landslide propagation and popularity of TM. Living from one high to another and one kick to another is a symptom of the restless generation of which we find ourselves an integral part.

People Programming

These days you can *take a course* in just about anything, from tole painting and organic gardening, to "how to train your dog." And government grants are even available for such obscure but apparently vital research projects as the one on "the perspiration of the Australian aborigine." Whatever the course may be, it makes one feel that since he is spending time and money, and possibly taking a course for credit, it will keep him busy and make him more qualified in some way. It goes without saying that a course in Transcendental Meditation fits well into this great, educational jigsaw puzzle.

And needless to say, the *endorsement of scholars* helps. Few stop to realize that scholars are not infallible. Very often a scholar in one field, because of his expertise, begins to become psychologically recognized by his admirers as an authority on just about anything. This kind of blind acceptance suddenly establishes a behavioral science scholar as an authority on Eastern religions and Hinduism. These scholars exclaim at length about the effectiveness of TM to lower metabolism to unusual restfulness and rightly so. But they avoid discussion of other methods which are equally effective, including one which we will discuss later that will totally free one from the burden of the faithful practice of Transcendental Meditation.

The "test tube" outlook now has a close second. Everything cannot be empirically proven; some things must be received intuitively, and university research in the field of parapsychology is on the increase. Psychic societies are multiplying, and it is reported that some Russian pilots are being instructed in ESP (extra-sensory perception). As a professing witch in a debate with a minister in Pleasanton, California, put it: "The Age of Reason is almost over. Man is now realizing that there is the possibility of supernatural power, supernatural intervention, and supernatural communication with the forces of the universe." One who reasons everything turns into a disgruntled cynic, just as one who spiritualizes everything may border on fanaticism. Real life is a combination and a balance of the two. Maintaining that balance is often a point of tension, but it's worth the effort if we can make a positive contribution to God and man.

TM's Impact

In the state of Ohio, TM has been incorporated into the educational system, and several other states are considering this approach. In Illinois and Connecticut, resolutions have been passed in the legislatures expressing appreciation to the Maharishi for bringing the Science of Creative Intelligence to the U.S., and recommending TM to the citizenry. This has obviously inspired the Guru—because he has now set a daring goal of one TM instructor for every 1,000 Americans.

Never have conditions been so ripe for the blooming of the Lotus of Eastern meditation, and the blossom has begun to unfold.

CHAPTER IV

The TM "Gospel"

Eager people, lacking in love, joy and peace, seeking a way out of the drug-abuse hang-up, and desiring earnestly a new level of emancipation by realizing the "true self," welcomed transcendental deep meditation techniques as "good news." The guru and master is the Maharishi Mahesh Yogi himself, who goes into an in-depth exposition of the "new way" in several of his writings, particularly in *Meditations of the Maharishi* and *Transcendental Meditation.*

The "gospel" of TM hinges on three basic, unproven (and probably unprovable by human finiteness) assumptions about reality and value: (1) the ultimate unity of all things, i.e., that all is one; (2) that the nature of the ultimate Being or unity is impersonal consciousness; and (3) that man's purpose is to raise his consciousness to the level of Being by means of meditation. These presuppositions stem not from behavorial scientific research but come directly from the monastic Hinduism of the Vedic tradition of Shankara. None of these presuppositions are totally right or totally wrong, totally acceptable or totally rejectable. They are, in actuality, vague half-truths. They have two sides.

All is one and united—in the sense that, by contrast or forced interdependence, man is obviously different and separated from God, there is a clash of natures. If this were not true, no religious practices or teachings would be necessary to raise one to a higher level of living with the supreme being. All human beings are not united with God, in that they are not in cooperative spiritual harmony with Him, simply because imperfection and disharmony cannot commingle with divine perfection and harmony.

The belief that *the nature of the ultimate unity of Being is impersonal consciousness* is common to most of the non-Judeo-Christian religions. For instance, the Hare Krishna movement does offer a mystical relationship with "Lord Krishna," though this is based on Hindu mythology, not historical fact. On the other hand, the Jewish faith involves a personal relationship with Jehovah God and points to a coming Messiah, and evangelical Christians claim a deeply personal, on-going relationship with a risen Jesus Christ as Savior and Lord of their lives, which makes it impossible for them to accept the "ultimate Unity of Being as impersonal consciousness."

Man's purpose is to raise his consciousness to the level of this Being by means of meditation—this, of course, results in a self-realization experience. If self-realization is what Transcendental Meditation techniques will achieve, it is hardly unique. For countless centuries people have been trying one form or another of self-help, of being one's own savior, in effect, by force of will. And dramatic results have been achieved. But again this runs counter to the thrust of Western religion, which begins with a personal God who calls for obedience and praise, both individually and corporately. Nor can praying and listening for divine guidance—what the New Testament refers

29

to as "the still, small voice of the Holy Spirit"—aptly be termed raising one's consciousness to the level of God (which, according to Christians, is what got Satan cast down from heaven in the first place). Rather, God, in His infinite mercy, deigns to speak to His children in a language that they can understand—a language sometimes of formed words, thoughts, or pictures, more often of nudges and checks in conscience and intuition.

Who Can Practice TM?

Anybody can. Have you ever caught yourself daydreaming or dozing (half-asleep)? Meditation can be cultivated, but it is actually an inherent native ability, unexplored by most humans who are caught up in the "rat race" syndrome. Meditators claim that constructive rather than destructive thoughts flood the mind as it soars to the pure field of creative intelligence. It is an experience that will recharge one with a new sense of vibrant energy and intelligence. Who can refuse that—if it is really available?

"The Power of Positive Non-Thinking," an article in *Newsweek*, January 7, 1974, records an amazing list of "Who's Who" on the meditation bandwagon. Bill Walton, a basketball star from UCLA does it. So does Joe Namath and cover girl Samantha Jones. The group also includes people ranging from Major General Franklin M. Davis, Commandant of the U.S. Army War College and twenty-five Trappist monks at St. Joseph's Abbey in Spencer, Mass.

Chicago's Upper Avenue National Bank President, Carver Nixon, is a Transcendental Meditator, who considers TM spokesmen as "nifty" and "very earthy people." Nixon's bank has invited the International Meditation

Society of the Maharishi to instruct employees and their wives in the TM way.

Charles L. Greer is an investment banker in Boston, Massachusetts. While at Harvard Business School he started meditating on the advice of a trusted friend. Greer's testimony is not unlike literally thousands of business executives who meditate on the way to work in transit, or at work, alone in the office. Greer regards TM as "merely a practical technique that helps him to cope with business pressures." "TM," insists the tweedy Bostonian, "is as all-American as apple pie."

The need for something to fill the spiritual vacuum and reverse the trend of human disillusionment is very apparent. The question is: can TM adequately meet the needs of all mankind?

How Involved Can One Get?

There are a number of levels of involvement in TM, if you have the interest, time, and money. It is marketed in totality; you as the customer must decide what you really want to do. You can read TM literature, view TV series and reports, and then talk about it with the neighbors like an expert. You can go a step further and attend the free, introductory lectures. Beyond this point, you will have to make a commitment that will involve you deeply—taking the TM course, perhaps even going to a school to learn the art of meditation.

The fall of 1973 saw the founding of the Maharishi International University. It received its first group of 250 freshmen—many of them college dropouts. R. Keith Wallace, President of MIU, with a Ph.D. in Physiology, feels that students who enroll in MIU know what they really want. Besides, the student gets more than an academic degree, "he gets a degree for the development of his consciousness." (*Newsweek*, Jan. 1974)

You may indeed be fortunate enough to achieve the state of restful alertness. "I find I need my TM, as I need my amino acids and my sleep, because it gives me a deep and profound rest," says Demetri Kanellakos, a specialist in psychobiology at the Stanford Research Institute. "Right now I have a stability in life that I haven't experienced in forty years."

Then there's *Newsweek*'s Religion Editor, Kenneth Woodward, who took instruction in TM and relates his experience. "I felt enveloped in a palpably religious atmosphere," he reports. "First, I was asked to remove my shoes; the fruit and flowers brought for the occasion were placed on a white handkerchief and laid on a flower-filled altar featuring a color portrait of Guru Dev. My initiator, a cheerful Yale dropout, then bent over the altar and, chanting in what I took to be Sanskrit, began a ten-minute ceremony in which bits of rice, salt and sandalwood were offered—in homage, it appeared, to Guru Dev. Suddenly, the young man bent low over the altar, then looked back at me with eyes large as glazed doughnuts. 'Hair-dhign, hair-dhign,' he said slowly, and it was a full twenty seconds before I realized that this, at last, was my own personal mantra—assigned to me on the basis of my age, marital status, and job. 'Hair-dhign,' I repeated, sinking into a soft chair. Maybe it was the incense and the flickering candles, maybe my own expectations, but soon I felt the onset of calm from the tip of my nodding head to the soles of my stockinged feet."

One can get in still deeper than that. In fact, a position

of a "priest-like" proportion can be achieved with "a thinly veiled Hindu philosophy, a treasury of secret words, and even a liturgy." To arrive at this station, you will probably have to be one of the fifteen-hours-a-day meditators, desiring the realm of consciousness as a vital and total way of life for yourself.

You may think you have arrived now. Not really. For the Maharishi holds that, in order to acquire consciousness of absolute union with the Being, it takes at least 73,500 minutes of meditation.

The Goals

An ego-gratifying goal that the Maharishi offers through the avenue of Transcendental Meditation is that of enabling one to find the God within himself. This again is based on two assumptions: the first, that God is in every human being. If viewed from within the Hindu tradition, this is a definite possibility, since the gamut of Hindu deities includes those who are good as well as those who are evil. Many of us human beings, if we developed our true selves to full potential, would end up as ogres. Other religions, such as Islam, Judaism, and Christianity which believe in a "good God" may find this hard to accept without some kind of commitment or conversion which yields one's life to this "good God."

In agreeing with the "divine spark" assumption, we must also believe that TM is the only means available to enable one to live a truly fulfilling life. And yet there are millions of people, whom we will discuss in a later chapter, who have found a level of successful and dynamic living and have no need for TM at all. In fact, some I have interviewed feel TM might be easier for them in some ways, but most definitely less fulfilling. So they have absolutely no reason or inclination to switch.

TM does, no doubt, offer easy and quick relief for acute anxiety, but it does nothing about going to the root of what's causing the anxiety; instead, like a spiritual tranquilizer, it offers temporary escape from anxiety—escape from the reality in which the anxiety-causing problem exists. Of course, TM does not consider it escape from reality, but a transcendence to a 'higher reality.' Unfortunately, unless one can meditate day in and day out indefinitely (and if one could, one would almost have to be tended like a vegetable by someone else), sooner or later one is going to have to return to that grubby, ordinary reality in which the problem still exists and may have even gotten worse in the interim.

Now to be sure, any person with a calm and relaxed mind is going to find that he is better able to "cope" with his problems than when he is in a state of mental and emotional turmoil. This is why we often sleep on a problem and tackle it the next day, after we are rested and can look at it from a fresh perspective. But quite often our own human nature is the springboard for our problems. Meditation will anesthetize your mental processes to enable you to cope with the problems, but it does nothing to effectively treat the perverted cause of most of your problems. It is like taking aspirin for a headache each day, without zeroing in on the real cause, which could be anything from a head cold to conflict to a brain tumor. Thus, in treating the symptoms of human problems rather than the cause, TM can be said to lack a long-term healing quality; in fact, in functioning as a crutch-substitute, it is actually detrimental to the building up of resistance to avoid future recurrence of whatever the problem is.

Incorporated within the list of goals achievable through TM are the following: cosmic consciousness, transcendental consciousness, and God consciousness. These sound rather abstract, but can be explained in simpler terms in the context of Hinduism and transcendental meditation (or the Science of Creative Intelligence) since these are inseparable.

I have not encountered any practicing transcendental meditator who can give a clear practical definition of cosmic consciousness. TM defenders parrot a concept from their doctrinal store which states, in essence, it cannot be logically explained; it must be gained by direct experience. If this is the case, that certainly puts it more in the realm of a religious faith than an objective scientific experience.

Beginning with the "cosmic consciousness" experience in the true sense, will place one in a vast, limitless, incomprehensible field of receptivity, even if one recognizes his or her unity with the "Being." The stage of "transcendental consciousness" is that experience achieved through meditation that involves the transcending of one's mind by the repetition of the mantra to the field of Pure Intelligence. The final stage of "God consciousness" is seldom discussed by TM instructors who are propagating TM as the "Science" of Creative Intelligence. The Maharishi, however, categorically states in his writing that TM is a powerful form of prayer and a path to God.

Is it really necessary to go through the stages of cosmic consciousness and transcendental consciousness to reach the stage of God consciousness? To those, like devout

Christians, who claim to have a direct access to their God through Jesus Christ (the expression of God according to the Christian Gospel), this process seems verbose, reversed, and unnecessary; they claim that they can transcend directly and quickly to God, merely by praying.

As one of them reasoned, "If I brought home a group of my friends with me, there are a number of ways I could let them in. The first way is obvious: If I have the right key, I can use it to let them in. Another way would be for me to go around and get in through the unlocked back window and then walk through the house and let them in through the front door. The latter is more akin to the TM spiritual ladder of goals and progress. If God is the Creator or divine intelligence behind the universe, He is naturally the key to understanding it. Finding the most direct way to get through to Him will bring us most quickly into a place of harmonious relationship with Him and His creation."

A statement directed to the attention of the United States Senate by John Tunney, Senator from California, was printed in the Congressional Record, January 28, 1974. This was a resolution in support of MIU (Maharishi International University). The resolution listed the seven goals that MIU aims to accomplish. (1) to develop the full potential of the individual; (2) to improve governmental achievements; (3) to realize the highest ideals of education; (4) to eliminate age-old problems of crime and all behavior that brings unhappiness to the family of man; (5) to maximize the intelligent use of environment; (6) to bring fulfillment to the economic aspirations of individuals and society; and (7) to achieve the spiritual goals of mankind in this generation.

36

The goals are obviously grandiose, (and are surpassed only by the claims of Christianity). Does TM have the ability to meet these challenges? The answers to these questions each taxpayer must determine individually.

CHAPTER V

The Experts Speak Up

Who Is a TM Expert?

How does one qualify to be an expert on deep transcendental meditation techniques? Is just being a practicing meditator enough? Definitely not. Is being a TM instructor enough? Definitely not. Most of the TM instructors I interviewed repeated in trained, sales-pitch style the materials they were responsible to present. The teachers themselves are first learners, and then channels through which knowledge can flow on to their students.

Is being the Maharishi Mahesh Yogi enough? From one point of view, most definitely yes. As the founder of the Spiritual Regeneration Movement, and the one who has brought into being in our generation the tradition of deep transcendental meditation techniques, the Maharishi should be considered an expert in his own field. Unfortunately, his opinion might be said to be a bit biased.

Let us look at some comparatively objective, reasonably astute evaluations.

Some look at TM only as a new trend related to the field of behavorial science, and for these the name SCI (Science of Creative Intelligence) is appropriate and appealing. Others look upon it strictly as a religion (variant of Hinduism) with no scientific implication. But a professor of religion will give us only a one-sided view of TM, as will a behavorial scientist. It is, therefore, important to receive a balanced perspective of the total situation.

Varied Perspectives

Psychology Today, in its April, 1974, issue, had a three-part article "The Facts on Transcendental Meditation." The article was authored by Colin Campbell, Gary E. Schwartz and Leon S. Otis. The article presented a very broad perspective, containing both "pros" and "cons" on TM. Colin Campbell pointed out that the concept of "transcendence" was very Emersonian (Ralph Waldo Emerson) and, therefore, very American as well. Businessmen are getting involved in TM not necessarily to relax themselves, but hopefully to step up performance. There are a couple of strong politicians who have been involved in the race for the office of President who are meditators. The public has recognized, however, that we must be careful in following in the footsteps of a politician these days. Critics of the transcendentalists hold that a typical transcendentalist is deficient in humor and a knowledge of history, and is very impervious to the realities of human problems. According to Gary E. Schwartz, it is possible for one to regulate his or her consciousness in an abnormal way. And then, TM is by no means the only way to relaxation; prayer and a time of beneficial recreation can relax you, too. Many are involved in TM for "kicks." Others strongly affirm that it is going to be of immense benefit to them, and are happy with their resulting experience.

Leon S. Otis and his associates at the Stanford Research

Institute determined that while TM could possibly profit many Americans, for a large number it would be a sheer "waste of time." It was also experimentally determined at the Institute, that plain "taking it easy" and resting for fifteen to twenty minutes twice daily, without any use of a mantra, could make you almost as relaxed as one who meditated with the use of the mantra.

There also seems to have been some possible misrepresentation of data relating to drug users who stopped using drugs after practicing TM. According to a graph by Otis, about sixty percent of meditators (selected at random) and twenty-five percent of people who quit meditating stopped using drugs.

TM—The Educator's Dream Come True?

Occasionally some parents in these United States are left wondering if some of our schools have turned into laboratories and our children into guinea pigs. Experimenting with our educational methods has taken on an almost fad-like quality. Properly tested and evaluated, educational innovation can indeed be beneficial, but TM seems to be fast becoming a popular fad on the educational scene.

It's one thing to hear what a young, enthusiastic teacher with limited experience and just introduced to TM has to say. It's another thing entirely to hear from a teacher with nineteen years experience, of which she has spent eleven years using methods that are every bit as, if not more, workable than TM educational methods. Such is the case with Mrs. Mary Rainey, currently in the process of completing her doctoral studies in Early Childhood Education at the University of Stanford, in California. Mrs.

Rainey is a specialist in Perception Programs and conducts varied workshops for teachers, and as part of her doctoral research is directing a Creative Development Center at Christian Center School in Dublin, California. The school is a private, interdenominational school with nonsectarian Bible teaching as part of the curriculum. Mary states she enjoys her work because of the openness and freedom to do what is best for the child.

"How would you describe your experiences with the utilization of TM techniques in education?" I asked her.

"I was invited to visit a Yoga school near Santa Cruz in California. After spending considerable time studying the techniques and their effect upon children, I realized there were some definite drawbacks, which strongly discouraged me from incorporating these methods into my teaching as an educational tool. I received much indoctrination from two enthusiastic school teachers who were transcendental meditators. It was noticeable that TM had benefited these teachers for a limited period of time—a year or so; but when a crisis hit they cracked up under its pressure. I questioned these TM teachers about the reason why they insisted I should 'mantra' if I wanted to meditate in my own way, but I never received a satisfactory answer. One TM instructor told me 'It's not important for you to know.' "

I asked Mary if she could think of even one beneficial effect of TM in education.

"Yes," she replied, "I can. One good thing TM does to help educate is that it relaxes."

I asked her to be specific about the drawbacks of TM.

"One definite drawback is that it is very temporary. In the cases of high-school students I have known, who have been trying to get off drugs, TM has been discovered to be a superficial and short-lived method. I honestly feel that it does not deal with the real problem."

"To what extent, then, can TM techniques increase learning potential?"

"TM techniques are limited in increasing learning potential. This is because they affect the left lobe of the brain only, the receptor compartment. The right lobe, which contains the memory bank, is not affected at all. Therefore, TM does not make lasting impressions. In order to accomplish this, teaching and learning must be done through all the senses. For example, a child learning about an apple must see, touch, feel, smell, and learn to hear the sound 'apple.'

"TM is an incomplete learning process. One will be tested in life in many ways, so over-all development is highly significant. There's more to life than just relaxing and receiving. Nor does TM give a child a definite frame of reference. There are few meditators who really know why they are involved in TM and not something else."

"Do you know of even one harmful result of TM?" I asked Mary.

"Yes, freedom without responsibility is what results through the TM way. TM methods are designed to keep the emotions in check, but this can be done more effectively through channeling emotional energies through exercise and discipline. Instead of TM 'numbing,' movement and verbal involvement can achieve a more wholesome effect, in that it is a more natural process." Mary Rainey says she uses chanting, too—chanting of poems and scripture. She also uses music from India, South America, and the American Indian tradition.

"We are not born into ready-made skills. Any skill has to be learned and needs to be taught. In order to do this right there must be 'structure.' This must be in an authoritative setting so that students know what is expected of them. For example, if you tell a group of children to 'line up,' they should know what to do to live up to the expectations. Educational TM offers no structure of any kind."

"Can TM change negative attitudes?"

"Even though TM may help to relax a student, it does not help one change the attitude of the mind and heart. On the other hand I have observed that the Christian framework allows people to experience this inner change, so that they can live life at a higher level."

Though people like Mary Rainey may be in the minority, there are undoubtedly other educators who share her views. What is the essence or the key or the principle of her educational approach? It is found in the "ground-figure" concept. Anything you center or focus in on is the "figure"—all the rest around is the "ground." Mary illustrated her concept simply by the "salt on the chicken" idea. If there is too much salt, it distracts from the chicken (which is the figure—the main focus). If, however, it is blended in right, it makes the chicken pleasing to our tastebuds. "Figure" and "ground" include color, space, size, and direction. Mary Rainey successfully encourages students to take Jesus Christ (God) as the central focus or "figure," and then "everything else will fall into its proper place," she states. The Creator should be of top priority, and then He becomes the key to knowledge, wisdom, and understanding.

I asked Mary if she had any verification of the workability of her methods. Without hesitation, she gave me three examples from her open and readily available records.

"Cindy, age six, a first grader, was unable in September

43

of the school year, to clap her hands. She reversed her letters and could not read at all. The basic patterning exercises were begun with her: crawling, etc., and work on her actual inability. By December she was much improved. By May she performed with a group in public and did a splendid job.

"Stan, a fourth grader, found he really had to exert himself to maintain a 'B' average. With the proper exercises and disciplines, he climbed up to an 'A' average by the end of the school year, and is now able to work with ease rather than stress.

"Tracy, a second grader, whose public school teacher said she was doing fine, ended up not being able to read at all. She was put into the program, and by the end of the year was reading up to her grade level.

"All children with problems in the school came up at least two grade levels in one school year," she added, "and these records are on file."

News of the validated results of Mary Rainey's successful educational techniques is regularly reported in local newspapers, and in early 1974, the President of Stanford University called Mary into his office to have her explain what she was doing. Papers she has written are now being processed for publication.

The Insights of a Berkeley Researcher

Dave Haddon is a free-lance writer based in Berkeley, California, who has authored several articles on TM. He has spent the last two years researching in great detail the Transcendental Meditation movement and has some unique insights to share.

"MIU," according to Dave, "mistakenly presents a

sectarian (Hindu) religious teaching in the guise of a science (SCI). Any favorable resolutions supporting the propagation of MIU will only encourage Federal aid for unconstitutional sectarian indoctrination in the form of courses offered in public schools throughout America. The zeal for the TM gospel, even though sometimes misguided and lacking in complete knowledge, has infiltrated the highest levels of the United States Government."

"What have you understood to be the purpose of TM?" I asked him.

"The purpose of the concentrated form of meditation of which TM is a particular variety is, in fact, to drain and clear the mind of all thought. The mind is then brought to a halt and left in a blank and passive state. This is referred to as a 'centered state' or 'cleared' mind state where conscious awareness is present but neither perception or thought is experienced.

"However," Haddon claims, "there are definite dangers in achieving such a state." And he cites Kent Philpott's book, *Demonology and the Occult* (Zondervan, 1973), in which the author writes that he has personally counseled people who had become victims of demonic possession through the practice of Transcendental Meditation. According to Dave, however, "the Maharishi cannot be unaware of such dangers, because people who are into meditation that may include any form of spiritual exercise are likely at some point to contact spiritual beings."

We have examined several expert opinions of TM and found that all is not as rosy as it appears to be. Now we need to take a close look at the Hindu tradition from which TM derives, to get down to what it's really all about.

CHAPTER VI

The Fruit on a Branch
of the Tree

Hinduism may be compared to a tree, Yoga to a branch, and Transcendental Meditation to the fruit of that branch. This simple analogy illustrates the deep-rooted ties that Transcendental Meditation has with Hinduism, and in this chapter we will analyze the "Yoga" sect of Hinduism from which Transcendental Meditation has sprung forth and burst into bloom in the lives of thousands of individuals.

According to the Hindu scriptures (Bhagavad-Gita 6. 20–23), "Samadhi" or "trance" is the stage of perfection. This comes about when your mind is totally rid of material mental activities by practicing Yoga. In that state of joy you will find yourself in unbonded, transcendental happiness in which you will delight through the transcendental senses. Once this point has been reached, there is no departing from it, and you will be convinced that there is no greater gain. Of course, you will also be completely out of touch with reality, yet from the Yoga point of view, this is not disadvantageous; on the contrary, what we would call unreality, the Yogi prefers to think of as "higher reality." He would consider irrelevant the suggestion that he has lost all contact with the sphere of daily human living, where the real action is.

46

Yogas—A Believe It or Not

"Yoga" means "union," and a "Yogi" is one who, through the practice of Yoga, has come to the point of achieving this perfect state of being united with the great "Being." Because of this claim of perfection, based on a presupposition and a highly subjective experience, Yogis have come into their share of criticism.

Many preposterous claims have come out of the Yogi tradition—the ability to walk on water, walking on live hot coals, lying on a bed of spikes, and others that Ripley's "Believe It or Not" has made popular. But during the twenty-two years I lived, worked, and studied in India, I came across little factual verification of claims of this sort. A past President of India, the late Dr. Radha Krishnan, considered one of the world's leading philosophers, said he knew of barely one-half percent of Sadhus and Yogis in India who were really genuine at all. In the language of the seventies, some would term them as phony. However, one must be careful not to write off stories of the kind we have mentioned as totally untrue. They have actually happened in various parts of our non-Western world in the past and still happen today. Yogis and others indulging in the release of similar hypnotic powers are obviously supernaturally endowed. In future chapters we shall take a look at some startling findings concerning the source of their power. Where supernatural power is involved, the effects may even be marvelous to the human eye.

47

How Does the Student of Yoga
Arrive at "Absolute Truth"?

According to Yoga philosophy, "absolute truth" is discovered as one goes through three different steps: the first is that of an impersonal God, the second is a more localized God, and the third is the Universal Supreme Being. The "impersonal God" is exactly that—vague and ineffable. The more localized God is often characterized by fancy idols that Hindus keep in their homes and worship daily with the mysterious blow of a bugle at sunrise and sunset. The great, all-powerful "Being" permeates every fiber and iota of nature and creation.

Many Hindus believe there is "divine" life in all creation, so pests thrive in a country like India, nibbling away at limited food supplies. Many in India will not kill a poisonous snake unless they really have to, in casé "bad luck" comes to them as a result of destroying divine life in another creature.

Kinds of Yoga

The diversity of Yogis and Yoga practices can get very complex. Krishna consciousness is also a Yoga discipline. The Bhagavad-Gita, however, describes three basic "kinds" of Yoga—three different ways one may abandon himself to God and realize unity with him. There is Karma-Yoga (involving work), Jnana-Yoga (involving thought and knowledge), and Bhakti-Yoga (involving devotion and worship). The three stages are progressive, and so as you progress, you get elevated to a higher level. How elevation and promotion to the next step is accomplished is not very clear. Another foundational discipline is

Hatha-Yoga. This is simply the "science" of mind over body, and therefore indispensable to Yoga meditation.

I met a lovely Hindu lady who came to see me about the acute family problems she was undergoing. I said to her, "Why don't you trust God to meet your needs?"

She replied, "I know 'Bhagwan' (God) can do anything!"

I wondered why this faith-filled utterance did not alleviate her sense of frustration or problem. Then I recognized the reason: She had no contact with a personal God on a personal basis. It somehow takes the excitement and enthusiasm out of worshipping God through your work, thoughts, devotion, or mind control when you realize it is going up toward an impersonal being. Knowing who the President of the United States is, is one thing; communicating with him on a person-to-person basis as a friend who is personally interested in you and your needs, is totally another.

Quit Enjoying Yourself

The Yoga tradition based on the teaching of Bhagavad-Gita discourages "the enjoyment of the material." You can probably guess how this concept would go over in affluent America. With the same fanatical propagation of this particular doctrine, TM would have experienced a "lead balloon" landing and burial.

Misery on Planet X

That there is misery on all planets is another foundational truth. Obviously, this could hardly be more speculative, but on the other hand, it is impossible to overlook the millions in India and the East who are desperately miserable due to poverty, religious superstition, and lack of positive faith, hope, or love. Many of these find it hard even to imagine an end to misery—life seems to be an unending nightmare, from which death is the only release.

About Leaving Planet Earth

On the subject of "death," the Yoga doctrine states: (1) no earthly scientist can stop it; (2) there is death on other planets, too; and (3) at death, after examination, you are sent on to a spiritual sky.

Many have tried, and some are still trying, but it is generally known and accepted that there is no scientist who can halt the chilling hand of death. A higher power controls the length of our lives and as to when we are to die. This makes for many the fear of death a plaguing problem if they are not in personal harmony with the Creator of the universe who is at the divine controls. For others death is a welcome relief and release from this life because they are confident in the future life their Creator has prepared for them.

The question of death on other planets is like the question of misery on other planets. If astronomers are not too sure about life on other planets, the question of death is irrelevant at this time.

The idea of an examination at the point of death is not really "way out" at all, if it is understood within the context of the Hindu doctrine of reincarnation. According to this belief, it is only the body that dies, not the soul. The soul of a person may go through as many as three million bodies before it comes to the point of being united with the supreme God.

50

When one dies, an examination scrutinizing the quality of the person's life will determine whether the next life will be an advancement, or a regression. Your "kismuth" or "fortune" plays an important role here, because it holds the key to the future life of your soul. This is what makes fortune-telling through palmistry, astrology, or other means such an integral part of life for millions of people in India and around the world. Have you ever considered the overwhelming influence of the "reincarnation" concept on Westerners today?

The concept of being transferred to a spiritual sky is an intriguing one, and is found in varied forms in the Jewish, Islamic, and Christian faiths. I think this is indicative of a vacuum in the heart of every being that only a higher power can fill, and with it goes the dream of a utopia—a place with a "heaven" image—far better than this present world. Pessimists would label as "wishful thinking" the imbedded hope in human hearts of a better life beyond the grave. But religious optimists who believe there is a future life seem to flavor this present life with more meaning.

The concept of a "Hell" is, of course, not mentioned here. No human being really wants to go to Hell. The word conjures up horrible images of demons, anguish, fiery torment, and excruciating suffering. We would all like to think there is no place like Hell. If, however, you accept the hazy concept of a "spiritual sky" with even the remotest possiblity of Hell included alongside Heaven, it is certainly worth the time and effort to check out ways you might get prepared for Heaven—just in case you reached the point of death and found out there *was* a Hell you could go to also, besides a Heaven. What if you did not qualify for Heaven? This would be an indescribably terrifying, traumatic realization, to put it mildly.

The Bible and its recorded teachings of Christ, the great teacher, have some very profitable enlightenment on the subject. Also, René Pache's book, *The Future Life* (Moody, 1962), is very balanced and scholarly in its approach. An enlightening experience awaits you, if you are openly willing to discuss the possibilities of "Heaven" and "Hell" with a Christian who is familiar with, and committed to, Christ and the teachings of the Bible. It may not be necessary, of course, but I have yet to come across a single religious leader from any religion who could categorically guarantee me that after death there is no Hell.

The Hare Krishna Syndrome

"Krishna Consciousness" is claimed by its leaders and adherents to be the ultimate link in the yogic chain. Without this link, Yoga is useless. All activities of Yoga are dedicated to "Krishna" (chief name of the Supreme Being). The Krishna Consciousness religious experience is meant to be a purging or a spiritual catharsis for the worshipper. This is certainly a mystifying claim, in that there is no mention of acknowledgment of wrongdoing or exercise of divine grace and forgiveness in the method of receiving this spiritual salvation.

What, in fact, it involves is chanting your way into withdrawal, and this is one of the key differences, at least on the surface, between Transcendental Meditation and Krishna Consciousness: TM at least purports to relate to daily living, even if all it does is give you a temporarily relaxed and calm perspective by altering your state of consciousness.

52

Chanting with Results?

Yoga devotees, chanting the "om" or "omkara" mantra in a subjectively involved way, claim to see an actual form of God or the Supreme Lord. Whether this is a genuinely communicative experience, or simply a viewing of Krishna's image or picture, is not guaranteed either way. In terms of making a divine healing impression on the ill areas of human personality, its effects on the individual and society around him are obviously limited. So, even if this experience does take place, it still does not overcome the sticky problems of guilt, fear, superstition, and human suffering. What have 5,000 years of Hinduism done for the country that gave it birth? Is there any other country on earth that knows greater wretchedness?

Yoga devotees also pray that they will not forget God. Yet it seems to me that the test of a religion that is really meeting its adherents' needs is that it becomes an integral part and parcel of the fabric of their lives. When this happens, it is impossible to forget your God; because He relates to you where and when you are really hurting and is never more than a prayer away, in good times or bad. You will not have to chant His name to remember Him; if you chant His name it is because you cannot forget Him.

Grappling with Materialism

There is lack of desire toward material things within the Yoga framework. It is a "plain living, high thinking" concept, and it sounds great. But can one actually divorce himself totally from the material? The answer is no. The closest you may come to it is through monastic living. There has to be a way to do it in the mainstream of daily

53

living, and that is the test of a universally workable answer—otherwise, it is only for a chosen few. It is possible—but only if one can realize the material in its proper perspective.

Some people look on money as a necessary evil. But it is the "love of money," not money itself, which is referred to in the Bible as "the root of all evil." Money itself is actually amoral. If used in the proper way, it can bring much happiness and blessing. Possessing money has not been the crucial issue; problems begin at the point when money starts to possess a person. The vision of life is imprinted with the dollar sign, or whatever currency one may use, and that's when one is willing to make self-sacrifices and step on others to gain more of the material.

Let's face it: Most of us at some point in life have been overcome by the material. Realizing we cannot totally rid ourselves of it, what we really need is freedom from the old perspective, and the will power to put it all in its proper perspective. Then we can use and enjoy the material without being possessed by it. Sounds idealistic? Yes. But I cannot delete it as a workable solution. Because it actually seems to be happening in the lives of multitudes of people. An old prayer from the Judeo-Christian tradition is still being answered in the life of those who believe—"May the Lord bless you and keep you. May the Lord make his face to shine upon you . . . ."

Is This Your World?

The material world, according to Yoga philosophy is (1) like a mental institution, (2) like a jail, (3) offers no relief from worry, and (4) has sex as its best form of pleasurable expression.

No argument can stand against the affirmation that for many the world is exactly what Yoga philosophy conceives it to be. They cannot handle the pressures of the material world, and are probably suffering from nervous tension and other forms of mental, physical, and emotional imbalance. Physicians everywhere endorse the fact that "a high percentage of diseases are psychosomatic." Fears, concerns, depression, and negativism are continually invading our minds and sometimes anchoring deep in our way of thinking.

Mankind most decidedly needs a new mental outlook which is balanced and filled with confidence, creativity, and positive perspective. And it has got to be more than coping with existence by relaxing and meditating; it's got to help you cope with your problems from a "new" perspective.

Because it is not long before one is "undergoing" instead of "overcoming" the problems of life. You are literally bound or jailed by your own problems, and almost everyone you meet around you seems to be in the same boat. They can sympathize with you, terrorize you, or ostracize you, but you will eventually come to the point when you will begin to realize the need for a super-human power to help you and deliver you from the "prison" plane of living. The religions of Shinto and Tao do not really even discuss this issue. Hinduism and Yoga philosophy in particular acknowledge it. In Buddhism we find Buddha saying, "I am searching for the truth." The Christ of Christianity's answer to this is, "I am the Way, the Truth and the Life. If you know the truth, the truth will set you free."

Relief from worry is an inward state, not an outward situation. Today you may, through various means, eliminate the problems that are causing you worry. Tomorrow new ones will be there to greet you. So you might as well accept them. Your troubles can be your friends. Your problems can be made into stepping stones for you.

How can you do this? Simply by relaxing or thinking positively? No. You do it by establishing a unique inward situation—one which is a renewed and workable perspective on life. Note: it must be *new*, since the old one was not working. Also, it must be workable; you don't want a bunch of static, intelligent-sounding theories. It would seem that if the Being or Divine Intelligence can create you or allow you to be created by His power, He ought to be able to do an overhaul job in you spiritually, physically, or mentally.

If sex is the highest form of pleasure for us in this life, we are obviously living on a sensuous, flesh level, rather than a spiritual level, and certainly this is contradictory to the Hindu concept of the God within us all. But one claim of the Maharishi is that one can enjoy sex more, as the result of practicing Transcendental Meditation. This is glamorously appealing to the "New Morality" generation in which we are living, one in which "sex appeal" is a top priority. "Sex," like "money," is amoral; and we need a new outlook that will put it into its proper perspective.

What's Ahead in the Spiritual World?

For Yoga believers, the spiritual world after death has light and eternal life. Within the context of Hindu philosophy, and in an effort to keep it consistent and non-contradictory, one must have both light and darkness in the spiritual world. The reasoning behind this is very simple: The gamut of Hindu gods and goddesses includes both good and evil ones. "Light" is generally symbolic of "good," and "darkness" of "evil." For example, it is hard to relate to "Kali," the goddess of death, with "goodness" and light, as she has such a destructive image.

The Four Commandments of Yoga

In the Gita, Krishna passes on to his devotees some "physical fitness" tips—many of them. It must be pointed out that many of the physical Yoga exercises have definite benefits, but Western calisthenics and modern physical fitness programs offer almost the same, if not more, benefits. The picture of a Yogi with distorted body as a result of Yoga disciplines may be humorous, but there are other ways to achieve physical flexibility and fitness. David Manuel, Jr., formerly an editor with Doubleday and an ex-Yoga fan, described his experience to me by saying, "I stopped standing on my head when, shortly after my conversion to Jesus Christ, it dawned on me what portion of my anatomy I was directing heavenward."

The four ground rules for serious Yoga meditators are: no sexual abuse, no eating of meat, no intoxication of any kind (drugs or alcohol), and no gambling. Note that these are the original ground rules. The Krishna Consciousness, and the Transcendental Meditation movement in the West, have undergone some adaptations in order to accommodate the Western way of life. The only rule for potential transcendental meditators is one that says "no intoxication of any kind." This helps to keep the system pure, since, according to TM instructors, TM methods work best in that state of being.

The ability to control both body and mind through Yoga is a promised achievement that has gained much popularity. If one is able to center on the "Being" by altering one's state of consciousness, then one is able to hold the mental and physical in check to personal expectation or desire. Yet again, there are millions of individuals who are leading spiritually-fulfilled lives and who have this control over both body and mind without the use of Yoga. We will be discussing this group in a later chapter.

The Yogi's Lot in Life

There is a lot about "Yogis" that is rather uninteresting and probably irrelevant to the mainstream of human life and existence. But if you are aspiring for a link or union with God through the medium of Yoga, you must know what to expect.

Yogis claim to have spiritual happiness to an incalculable degree. Sometimes the word "joy" is mistakenly used. "Happiness" is a pleasurable state of mind and heart in relation to your outward happenings. "Joy" more accurately refers to an inward state generally of a more spiritual nature. A person more relaxed through Yoga meditation will be happier, in that he will be able to cope with his circumstances, thanks to the "numbing" effect that altering one's state of consciousness has in relation to bitter realities.

David Manuel, Jr., of whom we have already made mention, shares a unique insight along this line. "I cannot recall a single meditation author or practitioner who is truly happy," he states, "let alone at rest in lasting peace and joy, regardless of the fantastic claims they might make. I used to know more than a few of them, and they were by and large lonely and uptight, and terribly worried that their books would not get proper treatment. For instance, I worked with one author who had spent five years in an Ashram in the Himalaya Mountains, studying 'Samkhaya,' and who waited obediently for twelve more years before writing about her experience. She was extremely anxious and insecure, constantly writing her guru for further guidance—and she happened to smell like unwashed socks (which has nothing to do with anything, except that at the time it seemed somehow significant)."

Since "joy" involves an inner spiritual state, your religion must make this available to you—if it has it to offer. The joy must be spiritual and working itself out in your entire life, so it makes you a dynamic person. It also must be a fruit of your religion, something not consciously generated, and it must be worth the trouble of having it. To date, neither I nor the researchers I have talked with have come across any Yoga meditators who impressed us with overflowing joy. Assuming they have this joy it could hardly have a lasting quality if they had to keep running back to the seat of meditation.

Yogis are generally cold-blooded, inwardly directed, and for the most part, totally neutralized in their ability to respond to human need or suffering outside of themselves, which tends to make them not very personable individuals. In one sense, this is a natural outgrowth of a relationship with an impersonal "Being," and a philosophy which holds that every man's present existence and circumstances are exactly what he deserves, according to the Karma he has accumulated in previous lifetimes.

Thus, seclusion, almost to the point of exclusion from life, is the chosen lot of Yogis. This policy of total self-involvement is designed to keep them uncontaminated and free from material desires, as well as being essential to their physical, mental, and spiritual concentration. This aspect is not a selling point, especially for the TM movement in the gregarious social atmosphere of today. On the other hand, if the method is workable, it is obviously rather limited in its usefulness if it is incapable of functioning in the mainstream of human life.

Have you ever wondered what happens to the Yogis who end up as failures? According to Arjun's question to Krishna in the Bhagavad-Gita, Yogi failure is a possibility. Failures end up spiritually fragmented like clouds disintegrated by a strong wind. Rarely, according to Hindu tradition, are Yogis reincarnated into a family practicing Yoga at some future point in time. They must wait patiently until such a lifetime does occur, and they must strive again to become a successful Yogi. Unfortunately, there is no historical proof that this has ever happened to any Yogis, so if you practice Yoga and end up as a failure, it would be wise not to stake your future on Hindu mythology.

In the assessment of any religion (and by now we have seen that that is what TM is), it is important to distinguish between "authoritative-sounding" presuppositions and responsible faith. A presupposition is one we are expected to believe in without a proper basis for its verification. Responsible faith is based on verified truth—a proven track record. Later on, we will examine a viable alternative to TM, which has a demonstrable and dramatic track record, but in the meantime, keep in mind that there *is* "something" or "someone" that ties this whole system of creation into one cohesive, cooperative whole. Regardless of what state of disorder and chaos in mind, in body, or in spirit you may be in, you still have fantastic possibilities to get spiritually coordinated and "get it all together." Hang in there! If you're openly and honestly seeking for "the best" for your life, you *will* find it.

CHAPTER VII

TM and the Roundtable of Religions

A Piece That Fits in the Jig-saw Puzzle?

TM is not a religion by itself, but a religious practice. How, then, does it work into or around other religions? We have already pointed out the TM movement's integrated relationship to Hinduism—complementing (and occasionally contradicting) its Hindu source.

The concept of "maya"—which means "illusion" in Hindustani—is one that is carried over into the transcendental movement, and in more than one sense, since, along with the realities of Transcendental Meditation are mingled so many wishful promises.

With "maya," of course, goes the lack of recognition of any real "sin" or "suffering." Why should these things be if life is an illusion? Let us examine just how well TM does fit in with some of the world's religions.

Buddhism—Suppression and Nothingness?

The man, Buddha, left many mystified and wondering. "Are you a god?" they asked.

"No."

"An angel?"

"No."

"A saint?"

"No."

"What are you, then?"

"I am awake," answered Buddha. His full name was Siddhartha Gautama of the Sakyas. Going back to the Sanskrit for the name "Buddha," we find its true meaning is "The Enlightened One" or the "Awakened One." Shaking himself out of a spiritual slumber, Buddha "woke up" to some life-realities that revolutionized him and his message to the world.

Approximately one hundred miles from Benares in Northern India, around 560 B.C., Buddha was born into the world as the son of a king. He described his own lavish rearing like this: "I wore garments of silk, and my attendants held an umbrella over me . . . My unguents were always from Benares." Today Benares is still world-famous for the finest in silk apparel. Things were going great in the cocoon of the courtly life until the unpleasant truths of the life outside burst in like a "spiritual holocaust" upon his life style.

Buddha was first introduced to the concept of old age as he viewed a wobbly, old, gray-headed man, bent and leaning on a walking stick, unkempt and uncared for. On another occasion Buddha beheld a disease-ridden human frame by the side of a road. Then, there was his realization of death as he saw a corpse for the first time in his life. Finally, he encountered a robed hermit, with shaven head and begging bowl. This, to Buddha, symbolized the life of retreat and seclusion.

Subjecting himself to the ascetic life, Buddha experienced self-motivation, mystic concentration (along the lines of Raja Yoga) and finally enlightenment under the "Bodh Gaya" Tree after a Wilderness and Temptation experience.

He was regarded as a rebel by the Hindus of his day, since in some respects Buddhism is a reaction to Hinduism. The religion Buddha preached was a religion devoid of authority. This was a reaction against the "Brahmin" caste (of Hindu priests). His religion was also devoid of ritual—he ridiculed prayers offered to powerless gods. Buddha preached a religion without tradition and one of intense personal effort.

Thus, a prince, disillusioned with the rich and indulgent life of royalty, founded Buddhism. Realizing the problems of "dukkha" suffering, and desire, Buddha is motivated to meditate and overcome the "evil flesh" until one is annihilated by arrival at the state of "nirvana" or "nothingness."

It is possible that some Buddhists may be involved in Transcendental Meditation, as most Yogis look upon Buddha as a "genuine transcendentalist." There are, however, four major points of conflict between Buddhism and Transcendental Meditation. First, the Transcendental Meditation school is not nearly as advanced as the Buddhist religious school. Second, Buddha preached a religion devoid of "ritual"; TM revels in it. Third, Buddha propagated a religion without authority; in TM it seems vitally important to submit to your instructor and eventually to the Maharishi's way.

Finally, their goals are different. The goal of Buddhism is, through meditation (mind over matter), to suppress the flesh to the point of annihilation, until one arrives at nothingness. The transcendental meditator's goals include "finding the God within you," "coming into the field of Pure Intelligence" and "Being," and then "living a totally fulfilled life." So you can see how the two are vastly different. They differ also strongly on the "God" subject, since Buddhism does not even actually acknowledge God at all.

Zen

When asked the meaning of Zen, an ancient master just raised one of his fingers. His entire reply was just that. Another kicked a ball. Still another slapped the face of the questioner.

What happens to an amateur who presumes to make a respectable allusion to Gautama Buddha? He is made to thoroughly wash out his mouth and never to utter the word again.

The following stanzas are quoted from Huston Smith's *The Religions of Man*, p. 125. This first stanza is supposed to express Buddhism in all its purity:

> *"The body is the Bodh-Tree*
> *The mind is like the mirror bright.*
> *Take heed to always keep it clean,*
> *And let no dust collect upon it."*

The author of the stanza is then corrected by the following quatrain, which is the Zen position:

> *"Bodhi (true wisdom) is not a tree;*
> *The mind is not a mirror shining.*
> *As there is nothing from the first,*
> *Why talk of wiping off the dust?"*

The Zen tradition is highly unusual in its claim to having a succession of men each of whom have imbibed the identical mind state of their masters who preceded them.

Zen enthusiasts are devoted to the Buddha-mind state by three primary means: zazen, koan and sanzen.

"Zazen" is literally translated to mean "seated meditation." Seated silently in the lotus position on two long, extended platforms in large meditation halls, many an hour is spent by monks with half-shut eyes. The purpose is first to develop intuitive abilities and secondly, to relate these to the situations of everyday living.

The word "koan" translates as "problem." One problem goes something like this: "What was the appearance of your face prior to the birth of your ancestors?"

Many of us would respond to something like this as a game, a brain-teaser, but Zen novices are not allowed to react that way. As a student is presented with a problem like the above, he then arranges a private interview with his teacher and this phase of the Zen process is called "sanzen." It involves discussion, deliberation, and consultation.

Both of the main sects of Zen meditation, Rinzai and Soto, involve the individual in attempting to actually experience for himself truth about himself. What a spiritual revolution our world would undergo if people realized what they really were, and then proceeded to do something about it, by taking the best course of action to change for the better!

No meaningless sound like a mantra is used in Zen Meditation, even though interesting observances like "quiet sitting" and "serving food," "riddles," "saluting and bowing to the 'god' in each other" are part of the discipline. The "enlightenment" state—that state in which the Zen student finally receives intuitive revelation—is not clearly defined and must be subjectively experienced, similar to the "Being" contact by the transcendental meditator.

"What kind of person is one after he experiences enlightenment?" an aspiring monk once asked a Zen master.

"His head is covered with ashes, and his face smeared with mud," came the enigmatic reply.

"What does all this finally amount to?" the monk asked further.

"Not much, just so," he was told.*

Islam

Around A.D. 571, a baby boy was born into the Koerish tribe of Mecca, named Muhammed, and his name meant "highly praised." Within six years after his birth both his parents had died, and he was cared for by his grandfather until the age of nine, after which his uncle received him into his home. We are told that even from this early age Muhammed's heart was being opened by the angels of God and filled with light.

Moslems regard the flight of Muhammed—the "Hegira" of A.D. 622—as a pivotal point in world history; from here they begin their calendar. Having to escape for his life because of strong resistance to his ministry as a prophet, Muhammed arrived in Medina. There, he soared in the realm of administration and politics; it was a meteoric rise, which left many astounded by his brilliance.

* From the essay on Zen Buddhism in the Encyclopedia Britannica.

The Islamic holy book, the Koran, is a "standing miracle," according to Muhammed, that God worked through him. Divided into one hundred fourteen chapters, the Koran is slightly shorter than the New Testament, and is used in the daily prayers of Moslems.

The most powerful and overriding doctrine in Islam is that of "Allah" or "God." "There is no God but He—the Living and the Eternal," according to the Koran (ii:255). Adherents to the Islamic way are generally strong in their religiosity and have no need for Transcendental Meditation. They believe in "God Almighty" and not "the God within me," and they feel no need for the Maharishi when they already have Muhammed, "the prophet of God." They are engaged in prayer, fasting, charity, moral probity, and a pilgrimage to Mecca as part of their religious life. Hindus and Moslems, especially in India, have often crossed swords, so it is natural that Moslems would be adverse to accepting a variant of Hinduism like TM.

Confucianism

With a sense of awe and deep respect, Chinese refer to Confucius as the first teacher. First, not chronologically, but rather as a mental and spiritual giant, head and shoulders above the rest of his class.

Born around 551 B.C., in what is now the Shantung province, he experienced a childhood of poverty and hardship which decidedly influenced his life's outlook. Greatly inclined to learning, Confucius rose fast in the ruling firmament, finally ending as Prime Minister. But China was a vast land of primitive feudal states, and he had no real authority, no chance to apply the elaborate (at that time) advanced system of ethics which he had worked out, and which was already beginning to attract dedicated disciples. These disciples did gravitate to the highest administrative ranks, and within a century of his death, Confucianism had become the state cult of China, which it remained until the Communist takeover in 1948.

The doctrines of Confucianism can be summarized into the five basic views of the founder. (1) For Confucius, "Jen" tops the list of life's great virtues. The word combines two characters from the Chinese language "man" and "two" and expresses the idea of love, unity, and person-to-person human-heartedness. "Jen" involves the dignity of the individual and human life itself, and the "man of Jen" embodies the humanity, wisdom, and courage that Confucius and his followers prized most highly.

(2) Then there is "Chun-tzu" which means a superior quality of manhood. This is in opposition to the mean and below-average manliness. Such a man must be a man of dignity and poise in society and totally free from vulgarity or baseness. Confucius believed that it would be the "Chun-tzu" people who would make an invaluable contribution to bringing about world peace.

(3) "Li" has a dual meaning. Here it refers to Principle, the Great Ultimate of existence, and in practical terms translates into the appropriate method of doing. This is evidence of Confucius's zeal to elevate his society to the highest possible level of living by doing things the way they really ought to be done. Obsessed by the idea of propriety, Confucius believed that a ruler should rule by moral example and not by force, and that the best ruler was the one who did the most for the well-being of his people, by putting the Principle of Li into practice.

(4) "Te" refers to "power" of the administrative variety.

Confucius leaned toward bold and humanitarian, albeit non-violent, use of power; to rule a state or a country not by force and violence, but by creating an atmosphere of faith in the system in its citizenry.

(5) "Wen" is the "arts of peace" as opposed to the "arts of war." Confucius viewed final success in international relations as the point when the art of statecraft is highly developed.

Cumulatively, Confucianism can be seen to be more a code of life conduct than a religion, yet a code that so completely permeated the soul of its practitioner that it would be an understatement to say that he subscribed to it religiously. It was to become the dominant philosophy of all educated Chinese up to the present century. (In Chinese, "education" and "religion" are the same word.)

Taoism

Some time between 604 and 304 B.C., Lao Tzu, the founder of Taoism, was supposedly born—"supposedly," because some historians are doubtful if he ever lived at all. He was neither an organizer nor preacher. In fact, he wrote very little. But whatever he did pen, he left behind as a legacy to Taoist thought.

The word "Tao" itself translates to mean "Way" and the message of Tao is contained in the "Tao Te Ching." First, Tao is the "path of ultimate reality." This refers to that which is beyond the scope of our natural senses. Second, there is the "Way of the Universe"—the force, energy, rhythm, or principle that pulls all of nature and the universe together, and gives it some order and coherence. Third, Tao refers to the way man should conduct his life in step with the natural universe. This final concept is elaborated to encompass the Taoist view of life which hinges on "power."

Magic is a suggested means to reach the power of the universe. The esoteric Taoists labeled Confucius as "psychic," and instead believed that Yoga-style meditation would be the appropriate means to receive the power of the universe, and in their religious observances they copied the Buddhists in most things, except that they had gods and goddesses for practically everything—stars, animate and inanimate things, parts of the body, ideals, etc.

"Wu Wei" is propagated by Taoism as a key quality of life to rise to the same wave length of universal power. The words simply mean "a total lack of unnatural action."

The symbol found in "water" also offers insight into Taoist doctrine. Water has the ability to float objects, to make its way through all types of environment, it has great strength and a way of creating clarity. It flows where it is most natural for it to flow, and it flows quietly, creating a sense of peace in those who gaze upon it.

Confucianism and Taoism are basically complementary systems. The former is a classical religious outlook and the latter romantic. The former espouses social order and an active life; the latter emphasizes individuality and tranquility. Their goal is "being superior" through correction and personal betterment. It could be that TM might fit into the religious activities of some Confucianists and Taoists, but they are already well familiar with its basics and have been for centuries.

Judaism and Christianity

These two are presented together, because in presenting the key concepts of Judaism, we are also presenting part of the message of Christianity, since the Old Testament (Jewish Scriptures) is an integral part of the Holy Bible, and Christ himself was a Jew. These two religions are as inseparable as the two sides of a coin. Judaism is one side, characterized by "the law," and Christianity includes that side, plus the other side, characterized by "grace." What the law could not do, God's grace to man, through Jesus Christ, accomplished. The Old Testament prophecy points to the coming of a Messiah for the Jews. Christians claim with abundant evidence that this Messiah is the Jesus Christ of the New Testament. Judaism does not buy that, and that's where they part. For Judaism continues to point, to search, and to wait for the coming of their long-awaited Messiah. Christianity will be discussed in more detail later; here we will concentrate on the basics of Judaism, in which Christianity has its antecedents.

What about God? In Judaism, all meaning begins and ends with God. The human race did not create itself, and human limitations to bring about what we see around us confront us with the real existence of a Divine super-power. Creation is not God or divine, but it certainly points to Him. The first verse of Psalm 19 (KJV) asserts this idea with: "The heavens declare the glory of God; and the firmament sheweth his handywork."

References are made to "other gods" in the Old Testament but it is quite clear that Jehovah ("Yahweh") is the one true God, above all and over all, holy and just. The first of His Ten Commandments, that are the foundations of Mosaic Law, is, "Thou shalt have no other gods before me." And idolatry—the worshipping of other gods—is as big a problem today as it was 5,000 years ago, when one considers how many things or ambitions or relationships we put ahead of simple obedience to God.

(Needless to add, idolatry in its most primitive sense, becomes a very real possibility when one considers the panoply of deities that stud the Hindu firmament and that will inevitably have an increasing influence on the TM devotee.)

What about creation? The story is recounted in Genesis. It was God who created the earth. He saw that it was good, and He gave man dominion over it.

What about man? Man has an eternal spirit within him that is God-given. But mankind is also fallen as a result of Adam's sin. When Adam and Eve deliberately disobeyed God, the curse that resulted from the fall has come upon all men and nature. But God, whose intense, personal concern for His chosen people is reflected in every book of the Old Testament, has also provided the possibility of redemption, a way of escape from sin and curse, first through man fulfilling the law (Ten Commandments), and then through the hope of a coming Messiah to deliver the Jews from sin and bondage.

What about history? Though God insists upon man having absolute freedom to choose good or evil, He nevertheless retains absolute control of what happens to the individual, as well as to the universe.

The essence of Judaism is in its Old Testament "Revelation" which speaks to mankind "to be holy and conform" to God's standards.

Judaism and TM could never coexist. Jews who sincerely believe in the Old Testament "Revelation" would find it difficult to accept the conceptual, impersonal "Being" of TM, the overlooking of the sin problem, and the absence of a Messianic hope and everlasting life.

New—But Minor Religious Streams

Have you ever tried to keep up with new systems of belief? With the recent foundering of technology and man's increasingly apparent inability to improve his lot, and the consequent resurgence of religious belief, there have been trickles of "new" religions. They may be new, in the sense of having been organized or re-vamped in recent years, but actually "nothing is new under the sun" applies here. They are streams that have meandered away from the major oceans of religion, sometimes with reactionary zeal. These new religions are minor, because they are fairly new to the roundtable of world religions, have a comparatively small following, and have made no major impressions on contemporary thought. Nevertheless, they are there, and can be touched on briefly.

The "person-centered" religions are those revolving around individuals—Guru Maharaj Ji, and Meher Baba, among others. We have already discussed the former. People who worship and adore a human being as god, guru, or master, always believe their "man" (god) is better than any other "god" (man). These systems have their own form of meditation in relation to their acclaimed spiritual master.

Meher Baba was born in Poona, India, on February 25, 1894. He claimed to have had a mystical, "realization" experience as a result of being kissed on the forehead by an ancient Muhammedan woman by the name of Hazrat Babajan. Eventually, he began a movement which today embraces some Westerners as well. His disciples dubbed him "Meher Baba," meaning "compassionate Father." He was very altruistic and humanitarian in his life's work, particularly in meeting the needs of the mentally deranged at a "mad ashram."

Maharishi Mahesh Yogi, who is acknowledged as "perfect" by some of his most committed disciples, does not directly demand allegiance to himself. He projects his techniques, but follows closely behind with Guru Dev and himself.

The teachings of Krishnamurti of India have a limited audience. Their focal point is that of an immediate self-observation. This way appears to be on the same wave length as TM's "self-realization," but it is totally different. Krishnamurti is a teacher, whose teachings bring "enlightenment" to his followers. In TM, self is realized by the altering of one's consciousness to transcend to the field of pure intelligence and "Being."

Then there is the therapeutic "Subud" religion, which pivots on the "Laithan." Twice each week people congregate in a meeting room to imbibe and yield to Divine Power. Each meeting which lasts half an hour may involve the participants in singing, dancing, sitting, or whatever, to express themselves and achieve their goal. No accurate count is really kept, and a gathering could range from very small to very large (in the hundreds). The movement was founded by Muhammad Subuh of Indonesia. He claims to be part of the "rank and file" of humanity and abhors being in the spotlight. The essence of his teaching is simply that self-surrender is the key to communicating with God. TM would offer too many trappings and "props" to a Subud believer; however, it is not inconceivable that one could be involved in Subud and Transcendental Meditation.

TM Co-exists at the Religious Roundtable

Transcendental Meditation, as a religious practice and a variant of Hinduism, seems to share something in common with just about all other religions outside of Judaism and Christianity. Let's take a look at how TM fits into the five basic functions of any religion.

1. TM, along with the major religions, is a "binding" or "linking" experience. We would like to believe that religion binds or links one to God Himself, but this is not possible when an "impersonal Being" is involved. So Eastern religions in reality link to a system of religious rituals, forms, beliefs, and commandments (do's and don'ts). If you faithfully do these things, you will find spiritual fulfillment because the doing will make you worthy of results.

If this method of union of contact with God worked, millions would not still be searching. We would have found God in a meaningful way. In truth, this is the cause of millions, including ritualistic "Christians" being "turned off" from their own or any form of religion. God and man cannot communicate merely through ritual; there must be relationship. And relationship involves commitment, communication, and closeness. Is your religion cold-blooded and ritualistic? Or does it relate to you in warmth and communion? Religion is ultimately a matter of the heart, not the head, and cannot be marketed in test tubes; so if your religion is truly relevant, it should make your heart beat with excitement.

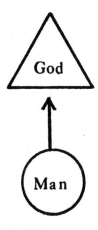

2. Transcendental Meditation and all the religions are an expression of man's attempt to reach and find God, or the "higher self." It is a reaching forth from man's level to a level higher than himself. There has to be more to life than the drudgery of a daily clock-work kind of routine. There has to be something more than man—something supernatural—to fill the inexpressible and unexplainable void within us.

Man has called on "Being," "higher self," "nirvana," "the Cosmic Consciousness," "the god within us," "mind over matter," "salvation," "truth," "goodness," and many other states and essences, names and expressions. Very often he has been frustrated in his efforts—resulting in withdrawal from society, in order to brood in active rebellion or in bitter resignation, or escape reality through drugs, alcohol, work, food, marathon TV watching, fantasy, madness, or suicide.

Because of human frustration, there has been an openness to any new ways that might work more effectively. Man has even tried to find this "undefinable whatever" by doing good deeds for his fellow human beings, that it might meet some vague "higher approval." The anguish of the search has expressed itself in worship of nature, fellow human beings, and profound and erudite sounding personal life theories. We have drowned our aching desires, at least temporarily, through booze, pills, spiritism, and other means. But we have never been able to submerge this desire to the rockbed of our inner man and just leave it there for long. Very soon it rises to the surface of the conscious self again, and the struggle goes on. For the heart will not rest, cannot know abiding peace, until it finds what it is searching for.

3. Transcendental Meditation, along with the major religions, focuses in on some form of "realization."

This "realization" experience could involve realizing your "self," the "God in you," or just enlightenment concerning human life. It's a matter of "you" being illuminated within.

And how one who experiences any form of true spiritual inner illumination loves it! It is an experience that revolutionizes one's life—for the worse or for the better, depending on your religious frame of reference. Realization is a form of progress. It is coming to a point and knowing exactly where you are and who you are. Realization can deepen or stimulate.

For example, you realize you have failed at a project—so you give up and quit. Or you can learn from your

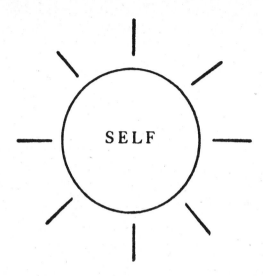

mistakes, so that failure turns into success as you apply yourself. Self-realization can be a "turning-point" experience—if you know which way to turn. Does your religion give you definite direction? Or does it avoid the issue, offer human guidance, or indulge in wishful, illusory thought?

4. Transcendental Meditation and other Eastern religions either avoid the bare facts of the human dilemma or offer no workable solution. Hinduism says it's all "maya" or "illusion," and Buddhism says one must strive for "mind over matter," until the point of "nirvana" or "nothingness" is reached. So here we have a realization of the problem, without the best solution available to us. There's got to be something better than struggling in anguish until you are finally annihilated. Islam strives to take care of human problems by prayer, fasting, commitment to the prophet Muhammed, chanting, and a pilgrimage to Mecca. But the outward "doings" do not take care

of the inward problems of "sin" and "guilt" that are the result of man's basic nature. Social and ethical systems like Taoism and Confucianism work through the medium of natural correction rather than a totally new, supernaturally given perspective. Judaism presents the law and the commandments, with a call to be holy and obedient. But the inner power to live an obedient life, to be conformed to holiness, is available only through the coming Messiah.

The worship of human beings, which we have mentioned earlier, cannot alleviate or eliminate deep-seated human spiritual suffering, since there is no super-human or divine intervention involved from the "Being" above the human scene.

Whether we acknowledge it or not, man's four greatest root problems seem to be of a spiritual nature. If we had (1) a way to expiate guilt totally; (2) the power to begin a new life in a higher plain of living with a superior perspective; (3) the hope that we are more valuable than dust to which we will return; and (4) the sure knowledge of a fantastic future life awaiting us after death—we would have a dynamic spiritual force that would overcome the earth. But that would also demand that the "Being" or the "Concept" we believe in would have to be ever-present and communicative—and above all, He would have to *care*.

5. Transcendental Meditation and all religious movements (save one) have been founded on the teachings of dead men, or men who are going to die a natural human death as an end to their earthly lives.

At this point it is impossible not to get a little subjective. I don't know about you, but I would prefer a religious hero or founder who had overcome death (for that would make him supernatural), and whose spirit of aliveness I can feel and have with me—so there are action and results, instead of pleasant but fading memories and repetitious, unanswered prayer. It seems to me that a dead god, no matter how great his ideas, cannot do an awful lot for spiritually dead human beings. I would like a God who is alive and will live forever. A God who just doesn't say He is God; but whose life and supernatural actions have left an impact upon human history and lives—and continue to affect them—and my life in particular. Not a God who is good at spiritual patchwork, but one who has power to make me a new person in body, mind, and spirit.

But along with all the good they have done, we cannot but realize that religions have also been responsible for creating "spiritual traps" for us—when what we really need is "spiritual release."

The author is indebted for some of the data in the foregoing chapter to Huston Smith's book, *The Religions of Man* (Copyright © 1958 by Huston Smith).

CHAPTER VIII

Spiritual Traps—and the Great Release!

Many of the popular space-age philosophies that are floating around are not recent concoctions by any stretch of the imagination; in fact, many find their roots in the soil of ancient Eastern religions. Westerners caught in spiritual traps may find this hard to accept or comprehend, because when we are caught in a spiritual trap, it is often the result of spiritual blindness, sometimes willful.

Reincarnation

In one form or another, reincarnation is enjoying explosive popularity in the West today. Rooted in Hinduism, this doctrine depicts all of creation moving in continuous life-death cycles. A soul may go through millions of bodies before it reaches the point of ultimate unity with the divine Being. The inspiration for this idea is the three-fold "Law of Karma." "Karma" means "work." The word "law" is not being used here in the sense of a scientifically proven and tested law. This spiritual idea holds that: (1) you *can* perfect yourself—though it may take any number of lifetimes to do so; (2) you and only you can atone for your previous wrong-doings. Since "sin" is an unfashionable concept today, a lot of Western believers in reincarnation conveniently overlook this idea; and (3) your present or future difficulty has been dictated by your past—over which you obviously have no control, so you might as well stop striving against your karma and go passive, "whatever will be, will be."

Of all the religions of the world, Christianity is seen to be in polar opposition at this point. For if you could perfect yourself, (and I have yet to run across anyone who has) Jesus Christ would not have had any reason to die on the cross. According to Christians, He, and He alone makes it possible to forgive the sins of the past as you place your faith in His finished work of Calvary.

As for the future, the Christian is faced with an endless string of clear-cut, free-will decisions: to obey or resist the will of God. ". . . I have set before you life and death, blessing and cursing: therefore choose life, that both thou and thy seed may live" (Deut. 30:19 kjv). No predestination in that choice!

God Embodies Both Good and Evil

Have you ever considered the vast spectrum of Hindu gods ranging in form from human to animal, and even a combination of the two? Have you ever read the Hindu myths and legends of the gods who came down and interacted with humans, and involved themselves in grossly human or ungodly acts? Gods both good and bad comprise the Hindu hierarchy.

Could you put all your trust in a God who might do evil to you? What, then, if you can't trust God? Then, the only person you can trust is yourself. The converse, of course, is that man, too, has good in him, as well as bad. This concept is highly seductive, especially for those who are obsessed by an excessive love of self. We can't bear to see ourselves as sinners, let alone *all* bad. We read of Jesus Christ strongly correcting the rich young man for calling Him (even *Him*, in his incarnation) good. Paul told the believers in Rome that there was no good thing in them.

The Eastern religions have come up with an ideal antidote to this strong and unpopular teaching. It is this: There is that spark of divinity—that little piece of God in each one of us—that, if we can only get in touch with it through meditation, we can raise the level of our consciousness until we commune with Cosmic Consciousness. Christians who hang onto that notion of a little bit of good in us that is capable of being magnified can use it as an excuse to keep from cooperating with the Holy Spirit of God who attempts to continually conform us more to the image of the Lord Jesus Christ.

In Christianity, God is all good. And fallen man has no good in him. Life is a series of clear-cut decisions. Hell and Satan are realities, and in ideal reality, the intellect is not king but submitted to the will. The will is submitted to the heart which is submitted to the heart of God, and the choice boils down to rebellion or submission . . . such absolutes infuriate the metaphysician who prefers to see everything not in black and white, but in infinite shadings of gray and who scorns the Christian as naïve and simplistic.

You Are the Answer

The "explosion" of knowledge in this century has been absolutely phenomenal. The increase in knowledge is getting harder and harder to keep up with. The ambitious attempts of varied and sundry encyclopedias are to be admired and commended; even though in many cases they only scratch the surface of what we know is floating around these days in every field of learning.

To many human beings the technological society has become "their" creation. Something in the subconscious pronounces man "master." "If we can do this much, we can probably do anything. Nothing is really impossible with modern man. If I don't have the answer, I can find it, because it is within the realm of my scope and ability." So speaks modern man, unconsciously "deifying" himself. There are many things we can do—but then we can't do everything in and by ourselves.

Millions of earth's residents are not "hung up" in either God or the Devil. Many don't accept or acknowledge the existence of either. They are simply "hung up" on themselves as individuals. For these are their own God, and the answers they need are all within their reach—a thought which gives them a sense of ultra importance. TM chimes in most harmoniously with this outlook, since we all (according to TM's way of perception) need only to discover the god within ourselves. I have yet to meet a single person who is excited, thrilled, and overjoyed about the quality of the "god self" they found. On the other side of the scale, Christianity is clear in this issue, describing man's spiritual state as depraved without the salvation of Jesus Christ.

Just Sign—"Sincerely" Yours

One of the most impressive aspects of Eastern religions is the unquestionable, ardent sincerity that emanates from believers. There are "phonies" in every group, but there are also countless believers who are deeply involved in their religion. I've seen them, the Hindus, dancing in procession to the beat of drums and the clash of cymbals, and singing with eyes shut zealously. I've been there to behold thousands of Moslems with skull caps bending their bodies in prayerful recitation to "Allah." I've watched the meditator sit under a tree by the hour attempting to transcend.

Since almost every Eastern religion lacks a strong, overriding thematic truth, there is some degree of incoherence, and there are literally hundreds of religious rituals from which you can take your pick. At this point it is not exactly *what* you believe in the religion that counts, but whether you are really sincere.

The idea of sincerity being elevated to a position of primary importance takes the pressure off one to believe in something that is worthy of committing his life to with wholeheartedness. You may now feel free to just believe whatever turns you on.

For instance, Jesus Christ made it quite clear that "what" you believe is more important than "how" you believe. He is "the Way, the Truth and the Life," and it does not matter how *sincerely* you or I might believe something else. We've missed the boat, if we refuse to accept "what" His message is really all about. Saul, who was later converted to Christ (Acts 9), is a perfect example of misguided zeal. Prior to his encounter with Jesus Christ on the Damascus road, he was sincere—but sincerely wrong—until he met Jesus Christ who set him right side up.

God Is in All Creation

The idea that God is in all of His creation is rooted in the theory of reincarnation. The Unitarian religion incorporates a similar idea. If a soul is impregnated with the divine spark, and this same soul travels through many different bodies, all of these bodies, too, will be filled with divine life and energy. So this puts God in all his creatures. Therefore, holy men in India are careful not to kill any living creature. It could be one of their own loved ones or friends or some other human being.

The Bible in Genesis makes it quite clear that God created everything, that it was good, and that it was there to glorify Him. However, he only breathed into man to make him a living soul. So man is the only creation with an immortal soul. He had the breath of God in him, but he was not God. Satan in the Garden of Eden tempted him to "be like God." Man (Adam) fell for it—into a state of depravity needing redemption. God is not in you as a human being unless you have repented of your past sins and invited Jesus Christ, God's Son, to live in your life in the power of His Spirit.

I have seen Hindus take the concept of "God in everything" to extremes, as they have worshipped their cash boxes, their merchandise, and the god in other people. Jesus Christ said, in the Sermon on the Mount, "For where your treasure is, there will your heart he also" (Matt. 6:21 KJV).

87

The End Is "Nirvana"

One morning, as I drove through the California Redwoods up Highway 101 North, I noticed that, crashed into the hillside just off the freeway, was an old brown car with the word "nirvana" painted on it with white paint. It struck me as a telling commentary on the "nirvana" generation—those who believe that it all is going to end up in annihilation or nothingness.

But for those who believe that the Scriptures are the inspired Word of God, the Bible is quite clear that human beings have an immortal soul, and that human life will end in death (except for Christians who are alive when Christ returns) (I Thess. 4:17 KJV), and after this death, judgment follows (Heb. 9:27 KJV).

It would seem then, allowing the possibility of the Bible being what Christians claim, that one is taking an awful chance, believing in nirvana. What if life does end in death and judgment for sin, instead of nothingness and annihilation? You would be wise to be prepared spiritually to meet God. Christ put it bluntly: ". . . no man cometh to the Father [God] but by me" (John 14:6 KJV). If He is right (and by now it should be obvious that I believe He is), then He is indeed the only way to God.

All Is "Maya"

Life is "maya" or "illusion" according to the Hindu scriptures. Probably all of us have, at one time or another, wished life was a dream, a kind of soap-opera world. But the fact is that that seems a rather illogical way of dodging reality. A believer in "maya" will be in for some rude shocks as he struggles to ignore the more bitter and intrusive of life's realities. (And we see in the cult of

Christian Science and its denial of sickness and pain the same sort of unreality.)

Jesus Christ did not die for an illusion. He died to save man from the real depravities of a human existence plagued by sin, sickness, and fear of death. Reality is unbearable without Christ, and as long as you do not have a relationship with him you will be a candidate for the "maya" concept. But His very real power can give meaning to the everyday realities of your existence.

Groove on Your Own Bag

This perspective is all-embracing, and stems in part from the "sincerity" concept. It is more than open-minded; it is broad-minded—so broad-minded that it is like a spiritual sieve. It does away with objectivity totally. Everything is "the gospel according to you." What's good for you—do it! If it works for you—do it! And let me do my own thing!

There is a definite, undisputed difference between what's my bag (personal willful desire) and what is best for me, but to climb to this higher level of thinking, one needs to exercise the power of evaluative choice. What do I really want in life? Instead of, what do I feel like doing just so that I am pleased, even if it gets me nowhere?

For many the "do your own thing" outlook is a "cop-out," prompted by a sense of purposelessness. It is also prompted by a lack of love: who cares what I do, anyway? A poor self-image is also an excellent breeding ground for this concept: I am probably good for nothing, anyway, so I might as well "do my own thing."

The trouble is, one can never go very long—let alone, indefinitely—without having one's will crossed. Then, by force of circumstances, one is prevented from doing one's own thing the way one wants to. Result: misery and bitterness. Viable alternative: do God's thing, His way. Result: abiding peace and joy, according to those who are into it.

Away With the Establishment!

Overwhelmed by a spirit of frustration and rebellion, usually beginning in human idealism gone sour, many have set themselves up as their own gods, whether or not they realize that that is what they are doing. This attitude is not new. The originator of it was Lucifer, the Devil himself. He rebelled against God's authority and was cast down from heaven by God (Luke 10:18, cf. Isa. 14:12 KJV). Now, when we are tempted to rebellion, we know the source of this spirit.

There are some Christians who claim that Jesus Christ was anti-establishment. This is an inaccurate perspective, both from man's—and God's—point of view. The fact is that Jesus encouraged His followers to render unto Caesar his due, and informed Pilate that his authority was given by God. Jesus Christ Himself *is* the establishment. As He said, ". . . all power is given unto me in heaven and in earth" (Matt. 28:18 KJV). You will never be anti-establishment if you come to know Jesus Christ on a personal relationship basis; you will become part of His establishment—the Kingdom of God.

Down With a Religion-infested Conscience!

There should be no dilemma that traps you in between "right" and "wrong." If there is, it is unfortunate that you have allowed any form of your religion to create in you a false sense of guilt. So say those dogmatic rationalists who do not have the courage to acknowledge their own past failures and to find a workable solution so they can start afresh. This is the result of too much religion and no spiritual reality.

What if we all suddenly determined to accept each other—and ourselves—in spite of our guilt, and say the best about each other? We would all be flattered, and our relationships on a human level would undoubtedly improve. But, this is only a surface improvement. The symptom has been treated, but I might still be (honestly) a "rotten" person inside with a "rotten" past.

There's got to be a better way of clearing the guilt of a sinful past than by simply pronouncing that it is the fault of some religion, and can be overcome. Because we cannot simply will to forget anything. There's got to be a more effective way. We've all lost enough money, sleep, and peace of mind over our past misdeeds. And TM is certainly not the cleansing agent.

The answer is obvious. We need loving forgiveness to wipe out the past and start a new life with a clean slate. Jesus Christ can meet that need—and only He can.

Christianity—the Great Release

It is possible, I've found, to be called a "Christian" and not have experienced the power of Jesus Christ, who is the focus of Christianity. This is nothing unusual; we have hypocrites in every religious group. For those who accept Christianity as "religion," that's all it is. But for those who have allowed the truth and power of Jesus Christ to invade every area of their lives, it is a dynamic, mind-blowing relationship.

Thus it is possible that many who are calling themselves "Christians" have inaccurately named themselves, if they have not been linked with the Christ of Christianity in a personal and real way. It is what man has added or subtracted that has polluted Christianity. In its pure, undiluted form, as contained in the life and teachings of Jesus Christ, and the acts and letters of the Apostles, as contained in the New Testament, it is still a powerful, unique, overcoming force. It can and will revolutionize you—after it meets you at your point of human need.

What makes Christianity unique when we place it alongside TM and the other Eastern religions?

1. Christianity is not a binding religion, unless we make it one for ourselves. It is a relationship with Jesus Christ. It is true spiritual freedom to live life at its highest level.

Jesus Christ said, "I am the truth." He added, ". . . and the truth shall make you free." When we realize what we are really like and desire a better way, we are opening up the channels for the truth of Jesus Christ to flow in and release us from spiritual imprisonment. It does not bind us, it sets us free. It's like this:

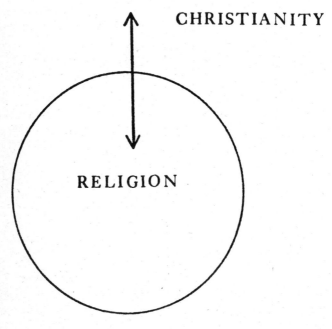

2. Christianity is more than just a religion; it is a relationship—a unique relationship, in which God made the move toward mankind. Because in Christianity, it is more than just a picture of mankind struggling to reach God. God reaches down to us through His Son, Jesus Christ—simply because He loves us.

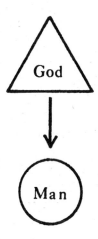

3. As in most other religions, Christianity acknowledges man's struggle to reach God, but it goes a step further: It is not just realization—it is a revelation. It reveals to you in Jesus Christ (and His sinless life), the nature of God. For He said, ". . . he that hath seen me hath seen the Father (God) . . ." (John 14:9 KJV). It reveals to you His love. It reveals to you that, through His power, you can become a new person and begin to live a life at the highest possible level. It reveals that, in and through the power of Jesus Christ, there are workable solutions to the problems of this life. It reveals that there is a fantastic future life after death for all who believe.

We've all had realizations, and they are often a discouraging moment of truth. Men everywhere are in need of divine revelation. If God is God, He will have something to say to those who honestly want to get into touch with Him. Revelation does not invoke looking for the "light" in yourself. It goes far beyond that. It is being illumined by light from above.

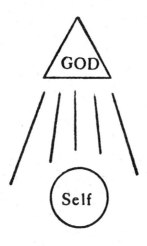

4. Christianity not only acknowledges the problem of sin and suffering, it has the healing, delivery, cleansing, and renewing power of Jesus Christ. Jesus Christ did not tell people with problems to look for a corner and meditate. He met them at the point of their need and by His power, eliminated their problems. He really made it possible for people to be happy, healthy, and spiritually mature. He grappled with the issues and emerged the winner. He promised to supply every need. No "altering of consciousness" was necessary; simply faith in His own power. In fact, it is a far more convincing process than in

many religions where one "tries" to move from experience to some kind of truth. He laid the truth out before mankind, that we might confidently move from truth to real experience.

5. Jesus Christ did die. But He was *raised* from the dead. More than five hundred people witnessed Him in a resurrected state. Some may debate, dispute, or deny this, but none has ever been able to successfully disprove it. Lew Wallace set out to write a book to disprove the life and teachings of Jesus Christ. The facts were so overwhelming that he ended up writing the book, *Ben Hur*, which confirmed it all.

Jesus Christ did return to Heaven, as recorded in the Bible, and witnessed by a large group of people (Acts 1:9–11). But He said He would now reside within every believer, in the presence of His Holy Spirit. This Holy Spirit is a guarantee that we are His, and He is still alive and at work! More than that—He is still working in the lives of literally millions of people today on a world-wide basis. So don't knock it till you have at least checked it out and made an intelligent evaluation of the situation.

If all this is available to anyone who believes and becomes a Christian by allowing Jesus Christ to invade their total being—do we even have need for TM? Why exchange a mechanical, drab, temporarily relaxing experience for an exciting, powerful new life through Jesus Christ?

CHAPTER IX

An Inevitable Conflict

TM—the Concept That Appears to Run Parallel

"Meditation" is an all-embracing concept with a sense of meaning so broad that it could include anything from daydreaming to receiving supernatural divine enlightenment through the means of relaxed receptivity. So, for one to say that both the Yoga-based Transcendental Meditation and Christianity agree in meditation, is both right and wrong. More accurately, it is a half-truth.

It is true that both agree on the need for an individual to meditate for his own good. But Transcendental Meditation and Christian meditation are two totally different kinds of meditation. The field of Christian meditation has always been there, thought it has barely been explored. The concept is, however, deeply rooted in the Christian scriptures, and we will be discussing it in the concluding chapter of this book. The important thing here is that Transcendental Meditation and Christian meditation are poles apart—and the two will never meet. They are two different movements in two totally different spheres of spiritual thought.

Pay—or Be Sorry!

If you can afford, and are willing to pay, the high cost of learning Transcendental Meditation techniques, you immediately become a candidate. If you can't—too bad! This attitude is obviously very necessary, especially when the Maharishi claims that meditating is a natural process and anyone is able to meditate. The reasons given by SIMS instructors for the large fee are the high cost of living these days, and the need for finances for future expansion.

It is reported that the income of the Maharishi and his organization in 1974 was more than 1.5 million dollars—a month. So exploiting the natural, inbuilt ability to meditate is obviously big business.

Is it really worth paying to learn the techniques of Transcendental Meditation, when, according to Bible-believing Christians, you can freely, by faith, experience the life-changing power of Jesus Christ? The fact that one does not have to "do" or "pay" anything to receive this spiritual salvation can be baffling and even a stumbling block to some inquirers. Yet when this actually happens to you, you will be a new, happy, fulfilled, peaceful, and energetic person—at no charge. It may be that you will eventually be motivated to help support the work of God, but whether you do or not will be strictly between you and Him.

Substituting "Another God"?

"Idol worship" may seem to some a bit strong description of the TM ritual at the initiation ceremony. But what else *is* offerings of fruit, flowers, and a clean handkerchief placed on a candle-lit altar before the picture of Guru Dev (the Maharishi's departed master)? This homage to Guru Dev and the Shankara tradition of Yogi masters is in direct conflict with the Christian concept which, in the words of Jesus Christ, is simply this: "You shall do homage to the Lord your God and worship Him alone" (Matt. 4:10 NEB).

Worshipping any human being or putting him on a spiritual pedestal is first putting you in a "falsely inferior" position. And secondly, it is depriving God of His rightful place in your life pattern.

For those, however, in whose lives God and the Lord Jesus Christ have not taken a place of central focus, worshipping or elevating a human being is no major problem. Some TM students have objected to the religious aspect of the initiation ceremony at first, but have later gone along with it in order to learn the technique.

Harmless Prayer Noise?

Some Christians have termed the mantra as a meaningless prayer, even though it has a pleasing kind of sound. The mantra may be of no meaning to the Western meditator, but, it has a great deal of meaning in its Hindu context. I have watched Hindu worshippers by the scores chanting for hours before idols during a special Puja (worship) Season, and I have literally felt the supernatural presence of the gods they were invoking. Even for those who don't understand its Hindu meaning, its repetition has a calculated, hypnotic effect, for much of transcendence depends on self-hypnosis to enter into the desired trance state.

Jesus Christ expressly forbade His followers to indulge in vain repetition: "In your prayers do not go babbling on like the heathen [non-Christians], who imagine that the more they say the more likely they are to be heard. Do not imitate them" (Matt. 6:7, 8 NEB). Even those who do not consider Jesus to be the Son of God, generally recognized Him as one of the world's greatest teachers and would do well to give such a strong admonition their serious consideration.

Direction—or Lack of It

Transcendental meditators are briefed, interviewed, initiated, given a mantra, and taught the technique. But what really happens when they achieve contact with the "Being"? Who is the "Being"? Is the "Being" good or evil? These questions are among those that the Maharishi and his representatives answer with only hazy philosophy and terminology rather than in clear, communicative terms. The reason: TM simply does not offer any "frame of reference." It is suggested to the meditator that he determine the answers from his own religious beliefs. In the interest of a quick sale without involving the meditator in the Hindu religion in which TM is rooted, no appropriate spiritual guidance is given. In fact, this unexplained, mystical appeal is a special point of fascination for many first-time meditators.

The Christian believes in definite direction from God, even though God may use different means to transmit it. The Bible is the chief source for spiritual direction. We must point out here that, while the Bible is a debated and disputed volume, it *has* stood the test of time. Nobody can claim to understand everything in it. But neither can anyone with an open, honest mind, who desires to weigh the issues objectively, ignore it. Its positive and beneficial guidelines are the basis for many legal systems in general, and the meeting of "down-to-earth" needs in particular. The Bible, coupled with the guidance of one's conscience and intuition, and the witness of those Christians whose discernment one has come to trust, together offer clear direction as to the intent and will of God for the individual follower of Christ.

Where, then, does the appeal lie in TM? Here: It is far easier to remain uncommitted to any frame of spiritual reference, than to commit yourself to something which may mean change in your life style. Because change—any change, even if it is infinitely for the better—is often held suspect.

Inward and Upward

The message of TM is coming through to a spiritually starved and confused generation, one that is once again seeking spiritual solutions, after an "Age of Reason" that lasted more than 150 years. Through TM techniques, one is promised that he will arrive at a field of "pure intelligence" where he can finally achieve the elusive goal of "self-realization." Pure intelligence—presumably that level of consciousness where one communes with "Cosmic Intelligence" or "Being" or "the Void" or whatever one's Eastern sect chooses to call it—is the equivalent of becoming God, which Hindu and Buddhist alike strive for, but which the Christian sees as the supreme trap of pride. This is the Lucifer sin, the desire that caused the most beautiful angel in Heaven to rebel and be cast down to Hell. God is God, and while we can be His sons, we can never be his equal. To think otherwise, according to Christianity, is to court eternal damnation.

Besides, self-realization is really a pretty limited experience, when one weighs the finite limits of one's physical, mental, and spiritual confines against the infinitudes of the Creator. Even though it might involve "God-consciousness" within you, true God-consciousness, beyond and far above you, that is available to His sons at times of His choosing, will elevate you and let you see so much more than just "self" as it really is. And at the same time, this freeing, limitless experience can allow you the possibility of receiving more of God's ability so that you can become the person you were meant to be.

Right On—or Missing the Mark?

There are four basic freedoms that will allow you to live a fulfilling life of love, joy, peace, and lasting meaning. They are freedom from plaguing guilt (available only through the confession and absolution of sin), freedom from ill health and diseases, freedom to purposefully follow a hero you know cannot fail, and freedom from fear's ace of spades—the fear of death. TM techniques may, in a number of cases, calm you so that your guilt complexes are reduced—but they are not eliminated. It may offer you physical discipline, but not healing from disease. It may offer you energy, but without a hero image and direction to channel it. Depending on how much time one can spend meditating, it may even offer some relief in this life—but no promise or hope of an ideal, eternal life to look forward to after death. Only Jesus Christ and His teachings claim to offer those freedoms.

Who's God in TM?

All religions are reaching out for the same God, but they are certainly not all experiencing the one true God. If they did, they could easily unite and all worship the same God together.

Within the TM concept, the Hindu concept of "God" comes into play, and within the Hindu context, if you open up your mind and spirit to "God-consciousness" via the means of the mantra (which invokes Hindu deities), you could be opening up your mind and spirit to the power of supernatural evil or good.

The Christian concept of God is "all good." Within the framework of Christian meditation, as we will see, one remains in a fully conscious state, listening for "the still, small voice of the Holy Spirit," and is in no danger of being taken over by an evil spirit. Which, unfortunately, is a very real possibility with TM, which is why the Maharishi warns the transcendental meditator against becoming a "spirit medium."

So TM meditators run the risk of being possessed by evil spirits. The way of Christian meditation presents itself not only as far superior, but far safer.

Bible Prophecy Encompassing the TM Way

Christians who have been following fulfillment of Biblical prophecy with great care stake their lives and future on it, convinced that the rest is bound to come true, simply because everything that was predicted until now has come true. God's Word has an excellent track record—one hundred percent accuracy. (The best that astrology and various psychics seem to be able to do is around thirty percent—just enough to keep the hook baited.) For a really intriguing synopsis of Biblical prophecy, Hal Lindsey's *The Late Great Planet Earth* (Zondervan, 1970), which has sold more than 7 million copies at the time of this writing.

What exactly *does* the Bible have to say about the likes of TM? God revealed His character in the Old Testament to the prophet Isaiah by saying, ". . . I am the Lord, there is no other. I do not speak in secret, in realms of darkness. I do not say . . . 'Look for me in the empty void' " (Isa. 45:18, 19 NEB). The mysterious secret character of Transcendental Meditation, its dark atmosphere, its searching for meaning in the "empty void" through transcendental consciousness—these are diametrically opposed to the Christian concept of walking in the light with the Lord Jesus Christ in complete truth and a sense of fulfillment. Christ is the Light of the World, and the Bread. He ends the search for you—when you believe in Him. He has an "open-door" policy, with nothing to hide.

Christians believe, according to Bible prophecy, that prior to the return of Jesus Christ, a false religion will arise, attempting to unite all faiths in a common but false political-religious system. TM is shaping up to be at least a prime contributing factor to this "new world religion" (Revelation 13). If you haven't already, you might have a look at the Book of Revelation in the Bible, and see for yourself, keeping in mind that the leaders and followers of TM will eventually be judged by the Lord himself.

What, Another Rerun?

Have you ever become impatient with a summer rerun on TV? If you see the same movie again and again, with each viewing it makes less of an impression on your consciousness. TM techniques help you to "cope" for a while, but in the long run, the crisis will still get the better of you. With regimented discipline, a transcendental meditator can alter his state of consciousness to achieve calmness and energy. That is his way of coping with the problems that face him.

But what if he were to become a totally new person by eliminating his root problems through some practical, applicable means? He would no longer need to be a slave to the repetitive TM pattern of practice.

The Jesus Christ of Christianity claims to do exactly that, and *millions* of lives have experienced it. If the TM way is claimed to be right and best because of thousands of practicing meditators, how much more right is the Christian way, with literally millions from every country in the world, including India (the birthplace of TM, where it is "old hat" and unpopular) who are experiencing the spiritual freedom in Jesus Christ?

Jesus said, "I will make you free." They are also completely satisfied customers, for Christ said, "If you drink of the spiritual water that I give you, you will never thirst again." Jesus deals with root problems and does a thorough job, once and for all. After that, you can move on—not in the same, rut-like pattern, but in a creative, growing, and maturing spiritual experience which brings new inspiration and strength each day.

Something which you must repeat every day may have a "curing" quality, but it is obviously lacking permanent healing qualities. Christians do not have to get relaxed every day to "cope"—because they have had a once-and-for-all spiritual overhaul. They don't need to become Christians over and over again. Jesus has saved and forgiven them, and through the enabling power of His Holy Spirit, they *can* lead overcoming lives.

CHAPTER X

"Where Angels Fear to Tread"— A Look at Some of TM's Contemporary Cousins

Unfortunately, TM is not the only consciousness-expanding technique available in pseudo-scientific guise these days. You can take courses in mind control, "clear" yourself via a scientology E–meter, groove into harmony through bio-feedback, even take an LSD trip without the LSD. Since they all come from the same bag, it might be beneficial to take a quick look at a few of them.

Take Off in Alpha State

Imagine a room with three bare walls and one panoramic window stained with dirt. The light from fluorescent tubes is glary. The room is strewn with empty chairs. Any warmth in a situation like this? Yes, only two thick brown carpets, and the deep melodious voice penetrating the minds of twenty-six bodies stretched inanimate on the floor. This is where newspaper reporter, Diane Shah, found herself in New York City, involved in a first-hand reporting situation.

"In a moment," said the instructor who resembled Tony Curtis, "I am going to count from one to five and cause a sound with my fingers. At that moment you will open your eyes, be wide awake, feeling fine, and in perfect health. Feeling better than before. You will feel no ill effects whatsoever in your head, no headache. No ill effects in your hearing, no buzzing in your ears. No ill effects in your vision and eyesight; vision and eyesight improve every time you function at these levels of mind.

"One, Two. Coming up slowly now. Three. At the count of five you will open your eyes, be wide awake, feeling fine, and in perfect health. Feeling better than before. Feeling the way you feel when you have slept eight hours of normal revitalizing, refreshing, relaxing, healthy sleep. Four. Five! (He snaps his fingers.) Eyes open, wide awake, feeling fine, and in perfect health. Feeling better than before."

"My eyes popped open," reports Diane, in her piece for the *National Observer* (Aug. 23, 1971). "I sprang up to a sitting position. I was feeling fine and in perfect health— feeling better than before.

"I spent forty-eight hours in this room, twelve hours a day for four days. But much of the time I was not in the room at all. My mind was projecting itself outside the four walls. I was in the alpha state. Or so I was told."

The literature sounds like a come-on. Learn to control pain. Dissipate migraines. Stop smoking. Lose weight. Relax. Cure insomnia. Improve your memory. Sharpen your visualization abilities. Become more aware. All through mind control. All for $150.00, the course's fee.

Whatever the mind dictates to the body, it will do. That's really what mind-control is. With a sense of discipline and purpose one must educate his mind so that it can be used to transcend one into the alpha state of awareness. This is, in essence, the mind control philosophy.

What can we conclude? The alpha state points up the most dramatic danger of deliberately opening one's mind. Originally, part of the technique actually included inviting "counselors" into one's mental lab, though presumably, through the screening of "The Exorcist" and the popularity of the deliverance ministry, too many people have become aware of the possibility of demonic possession. The danger is no less imminent.

Laboratory-Style Mysticism

The "brain-mind system" has a built-in contact into the Ultimate Being. That's the conclusion of Dr. Robert E. L. Masters, forty, and Dr. Jean Houston, thirty-one, on the basis of hundreds of experiments they have conducted in their Foundation for Mind Research, in New York City.

In a *Time* magazine article, "Mysticism in the Laboratory" (Oct. 5, 1971), religion researcher, Clare Mead, reports some unusual sensations she experienced during a half-hour odyssey of autosuggestion.

"At Dr. Houston's suggestion, I began 'flying' . . . to the center of my being, and finally to the core of life itself." Miss Mead describes the images she encountered there, then continues, "At this point, Dr. Houston decided I was able to undergo a psychological 'death' and 're-birth'. . . . Eventually, I had to restrain myself from sheer bawling. I knew objectively that I was sitting there alive and well in a room in Upper Manhattan, but subjectively the sensation of death was as vivid as if I were looking into my own coffin."

An LSD trip without LSD?

Empowered By a Precision Instrument

Bio-feedback is fast becoming a unique technological device for the developing of mental, physical, and emotional controls.

What are the wonders of the electroencephalograph? Originally intended by medical science to detect eccentricities in the minute electrical charges put out by the brain, and thus indicate possible abnormalities in the brain's function, it is used to present the bio-feedback student with a performance report of how he is progressing in using mind power to control the physical and emotional outputs, as well as to cultivate a creative attitude.

In order to develop calmness and relaxation, affirmations or "autogenic" statements are used in bio-feedback —statements that ring with attitudes like faith, love, hope, peace, and healing.

Bio-feedback practitioners assert that the equipment used does not make contact with spiritual forces. However, there is feedback related to one's development of relaxation (alpha waves), creativity and deep meditation (theta waves), and the edge of cosmic consciousness (delta waves) that result from a detachment.

A student can adjust his development and maturity according to the need. Disease, chaos, unusual stress, and plaguing questions may need more time in the machine. The better you get on the machine, the sooner you can get off it, supposedly. The equipment is now used on people to assist them in the cure of migraine headaches, tension, epilepsy, and gastrointestinal disorders.

What does the future look like? Tests are underway to find out whether it can offer aid in curing cancer, arthritis, muscular disorders, hypertension, and heart palpitations. After all, it will not hurt anyone because the equipment is not electrical, but battery operated. And, along with the electroencephalograph there is the electromyograph to give you feedback on muscular tension.

Some believe that bio-feedback is going to be the next "in" thing. And they may be right. On a closer examination of its power source, we will soon realize that it is another phase of unleashing soul force through self-hypnosis. And, by the way, who is the "divine" being who you can contact? We'll get into that.

The Power of the Mantra

One of the main purposes of the mantra is to aid the process of self-hypnosis, which is what TM really is. Doctors are now validating the astonishing power of the mind to make the body do exactly what it dictates under hypnosis, but with hypnosis becoming less and less essential—from lowering one's body temperature by a precise fifth of a degree, to accelerating or retarding one's pulse rate. Where does this fantastic latent ability come from? The fact is that Western scientists are realizing that they've only tapped the surface, and the ramifications are enormous . . . but to the Hindu, the notion of mind over everything is old hat.

The mantra is an aid to self-hypnosis, and several Eastern religions also employ its visual counterpart, the "mandala." This is an intricate abstract design, at which one stares while repeating one's mantra. They are often quite elaborate and arabesque, but since self-hypnosis is the ultimate goal, any fixed, visual focal point will do—a candle, an orange dot on a blue background, a crystal ball, even a photo of Guru Dev.

There Are Hindu "Fakers" As Well As Genuine Hindu "Fakirs"

There are too many Christian eyewitness accounts of their feats not to credit them, and these same scientists who are experimenting with hypnosis acknowledge their plausibility. And just as a reminder to us that they are but counterfeits of God's power, there is the story in Joe Donato's book, *Tell it to the Mafia* (Logos, 1975), of the hypnotist who could not burn Joe's fingers with a butane lighter. There is indeed a psychic power that can be unleashed through hypnosis, but it comes from the soul not the spirit, and it is certainly not of the Holy Spirit.

Zeroing in on the Power Source

Watchman Nee, Chinese Christian scholar, highlights some key concepts in *The Latent Power of the Soul* (Christian Fellowship Publishers, 1972), related to the power source in mind-control exercises, whether they are religious or non-religious.

Biblical passages establish the trilogy of the spirit, soul, and body—the components that go together to form "you" or "me" as human beings. Genesis 2:7 refers to the human body recording the fact that "God formed man of the dust of the ground" (KJV). God then "breathed into his nostrils the breath of life." This is a reference to the "spirit." It was only after that, that man became "a living soul." Watchman Nee expresses it this way:

According to common understanding the soul is our personality. When the spirit and the body were joined, man became a living soul. The characteristic of the angels is spirit and that of the lower animals such as beasts is flesh. We humans have both spirit and body; but our characteristic is neither spirit nor body but soul. We have a living soul. Hence the Bible calls man soul. For example, when Jacob went down into Egypt with his family, the Scriptures tell us that "all the souls of the house of Jacob, that came into Egypt, were threescore and ten" (Gen. 46.27). Again, those who had received Peter's word on Pentecost were baptised and "there were added unto them in that day about three thousand souls" (Acts 2.41). Hence soul stands for our personality, for what makes us as man.

In one sense, every human being was meant to be a meditator and get "linked". The spirit links us to God, the soul to ourselves, and the body to the world in which we live. Nee notes that, in his reference Bible, C. I. Scofield explains that the spirit gives God-consciousness, the soul self-consciousness, the body world-consciousness.

The Genesis story of man's marvelous God, who gives abilities and responsibilities, is familiar to us. But then Adam and the human race "fell." The "living soul" now is referred to as "flesh" or "human" being for several passages, including Romans 3:20 (KJV) which reads: ". . . by the deeds of the law there shall no flesh be justified in His sight . . ."

Man is referred to as a "lost soul" and his power is latent rather than active. It is bound up in the flesh. Jesus

Christ came to save the human "soul," by giving man a new spirit (Ezek. 36:26 KJV).

Man's soul is a battlefield for the forces of God and Christ (good), and Satan, the Devil (evil). Satan, the enemy of God and mankind, attempts to release the fallen soul's power, as individuals open up to supernatural forces other than that of Jesus Christ. This results in psychic and maybe miraculous abilities that give glory to self and indirectly to Satan, instead of to Jesus Christ.

This is a heavy concept for one, who is looking within, to accept. For even many Christians are duped to accept this soul power as being "of God." The Holy Spirit works in our renewed Spirit, and this is God's method. Jesus declares the importance of losing one's self (soul), so He can renew us to live a life in the Spirit. That which is then accomplished by God, in response to prayer, is indeed miraculous, and has nothing whatever to do with us. It is a manifestation of the power of the Holy Spirit, as opposed to soul power, that psychic force which is unleashed from man's own soul.

All religions caught up in mind-control and hypnosis syndromes zero in on disciplining or subjecting the flesh, so as to release this soul power. Some may use sophisticated instruments and intellectually-appealing jargon to accomplish it, whether it be through self-inflicted asceticism, abstract meditation, the "maya" outlook, or some other method. Waiting in the alpha state and passively opening up your mind to whatever "counselor" happens to come up the elevator is fine—if you are ready to accept the soul force released by the Devil himself. At least the psychic experimenters are honest about what they are trying to do—though they are embarrassed at any association with occultists, who, in turn, are embarrassed at being compared with Satanists who have no illusions about who—or what—they are conjuring up. But they are all interested in the same thing: supernatural power. And the big lie that all (save the Satanists) believe is that supernatural power can emanate from a "neutral" source, and can be controlled by man for "good."

The truth is that there is no supernatural no-man's-land, no spiritual vacuum, any more than reality is a shading of grays, rather than a series of black-and-white choices. Supernatural power comes either from God, and may be influenced—but cannot be controlled—by prayer; or it comes from Satan, either directly, through Satanic or demonic intervention, or indirectly, through the release of forbidden soul force. Man may think he is in control of himself and his "psychic ability," but the fact is, Satan is running anyone who is not being run by God (i.e., living in obedience to His continuing will).

Franz Anton Mesmer, the father of modern parapsychology, discovered in 1778, what was originally referred to as "mesmerism" and is today known as hypnotism. This has been called the soul-bed from which many mental sciences have sprung forth in the West, since all of them use hypnotism in one form or another.

It is interesting to note that the Bible expressly forbids "charming" and "enchanting" (or "casting of spells," in the New American Standard translation), which certainly encompasses modern hypnotism, putting hypnotists in the same bag with witches, diviners (psychics), consulters with familiar spirits (mediums), observers of time (astrologers) and necromancers (spiritists). These "innocent" occult practices are considered nothing less than an abomination in the sight of the Lord, as Deuteronomy 18 and Leviticus 19 make abundantly clear.

The new birth experience of becoming a Christian, that anyone can experience as described in John 3:6, is clearly highlighted: ". . . that which is born of the Spirit is spirit" (KJV). God works in the spirit of man, by His Spirit (in Greek, *pneuma*). Satan works in the soul (*psyche*). At the point of accepting Jesus Christ, a Christian's soul is brought under subjection to His Spirit. God fills our spirit with His Holy Spirit. But, we must live with the old man (the soulish nature) till we die; and so we may let our souls be a point of vantage for Satan, if we are not careful.

There are three reasons Satan wants to see as many people as possible embrace voluntary passivity: (1) it effectively neutralizes any "redeeming social value" they might have (let alone lessening the possibility of their becoming Christians), and instead causes them to become a burden to mankind; (2) it opens them to direct manipulation, either demonic or by means of Satanic "revelation"; and (3) it releases their soul force and makes it available to the enemy, for his purposes.

How, then, can we discern the difference between the power of God, and the power of the Devil? It's not too hard: God is good. But for the Devil, "evil" appearance is not the only criterion. He uses "the gray area"—things seemingly "good" or "neutral," and it is here that we find ourselves in need of a yardstick of some kind. Especially when soul force is not always "harmful" to the human eye. In fact, it is being praised as "helpful" in releasing some much-needed answers.

But there is a deception here. We need to distinguish

114

between the Spirit of truth (in Jesus Christ) and the spirit of error (soul-power released by the Devil). Here is a conclusive testimony on the question at hand:

> *But do not trust any and every spirit, my friends; test the spirits, to see whether they are from God, for among those who have gone out into the world there are many prophets falsely inspired. This is how we may recognize the Spirit of God: every spirit which acknowledges that Jesus Christ has come in the flesh is from God, and every spirit which does not thus acknowledge Jesus is not from God. This is what is meant by 'Antichrist'; you have been told that he was to come, and here he is, in the world already!*
>
> *But you, my children, are of God's family, and you have the mastery over these false prophets, because he who inspires you is greater than he who inspires the godless world. They are of that world, and so therefore is their teaching; that is why the world listens to them. But we belong to God, and a man who knows God listens to us, while he who does not belong to God refuses us a hearing. That is how we distinguish the spirit of truth from the spirit of error* (I John 4:1–6 NEB).

We are living in the times when the trading in human souls is big business, for the dissemination of much latent soul-power is at stake in the Christless, mind-control techniques. Revelation 18:11–13 lists goods to be bought and sold by merchants in the end times. The list includes gold, silver, cattle, slaves, and "human souls."

The first step toward spiritual fulfillment and fruitfulness through the power of Jesus Christ and His Spirit is a total rejection of psychic and soul forces.

CHAPTER XI

Turned Off . . . and On!

The Word of Some Who Have Tried TM

What turned Vail Hamilton to Transcendental Meditation? "Were you really that impressed by it?" I asked.

"Yes," replied Vail, "I really was. I was very impressed by a lecture of Jerry Jarvis. More than his lecture, he gave the impression of relaxed poise and obvious peacefulness. You could see results in his life. He seemed to have the evidence. By contrast, I was suffering from a state of purposelessness, meaningless living, and heading toward spiritual disintegration. I thought TM would help me get myself together. I was searching for God and wanted some kind of experience with the Lord."

Vail Hamilton is thirty-one but looks twenty-six, and is a graduate of the University of California, Berkeley, with a major in Art. She was born in Princeton, New Jersey, but has lived in California for most of her life. Vail has been a transcendental meditator for five years, of which for one year she was a SIMS instructor.

"I was immensely perturbed by the deception aspect of TM instruction," she continued. "In the guise of a relaxing technique, as an instructor I had to withhold information from the students I was teaching, and then, when they were sucked in, I involved them in the religious aspects of TM. The mantra and the Hindu initiation ceremony really bothered me. They were not only religious, but were misrepresented as a 'Creative Intelligence Science' and a mental technique. Moreover, student meditators are not to be told immediately by the SIMS instructors that, at a later state, they would be moving into 'cosmic consciousness' and 'God-consciousness.' "

I asked Vail about the initiation ceremony.

"The initiation ceremony is inexorably linked with the Shankara tradition of Hinduism. In a candle-lit, eerie atmosphere, with an offering, I sang a hymn of praise to the Hindu master, and gave each candidate his or her mantra. Every transcendental meditator must participate in this ritual before the image of Guru Dev, the Maharishi's departed master. In fact, the Maharishi considers this a 'holy tradition'—one that is not merely held in high regard, but has come to be actually worshipped by seekers of truth and knowers of reality."

I had heard that in the transcendental trance, outside influences did indeed make themselves known, and I asked about them. "In some forms of expansive meditational practices, meditators experience the presence of supernatural phenomena, appearing in the form of gods, demons, or monsters. Did you ever have an experience of this type?"

"Yes, I did. We were advised not to pay any attention to them, no matter in what form they appeared. As an instructor I was told to tell meditators to leave these supernatural beings alone, and to go on with their own business. But I will never forget my experiencing the presence of supernatural spirits."

Vail then shared an interesting insight about the

assigned mantra. What she said was really no different from what my Bengali (language of Eastern India) teacher, Binal Kumar Pal, told me about Hindu worship. He stated that as worshippers chanted and danced to the beat of drums before the idols of whatever Hindu god was in season (they have several different "Puja" or "worship" seasons in India), the spirit of this particular god infused the entire being of the worshipper. There is "Kali," the goddess of death, 'Saraswati,' the goddess of wealth, and scores of other gods and goddesses.

"It was not long before I realized that I had to find 'The Truth' outside of Transcendental Meditation. While a student at the University of California, I encountered John Panama. John Panama is a Berkeley resident who has reportedly been into all kinds of spiritual trips. I attended a group that he organized to engage in group meditation. John asked them (most of them came to the group with some spiritual experience under their belts) to try chanting to different names and beings, to see what kind of sensations may be experienced with each mantra that was chanted.

"First he asked the group to chant the name of the best friend each one of them had. And we did so. Then, he read off a list of names of religious leaders for chanting— Krishna, Buddha, and Jesus Christ. All of us meditators made it through 'Krishna' and 'Buddha.' But when we came to 'Jesus,' we were unable to audibly and clearly mouth the words. John Panama told us that he was convinced that Jesus could give us more than a blissful sensation; He could give us purity. He was presented as 'the remedy' for a guilt-filled conscience. I could barely say 'Jesus,' but I kept trying and opening my heart and mind to Him as I did.

"By calling upward and outward to Jesus to meet my

119

heart's cry, I experienced His love, forgiveness, peace, and joy. And the more I experienced, the more I called out. On the seventh day of calling out, I received the Baptism in the Holy Spirit (the total immersion in the fullness of His Spirit)." I asked Vail if, after becoming a Christian, she continued to be involved in TM. After all, having been in it for so long, it had probably become second nature to her.

"Not long after I accepted Jesus Christ into the fabric of my life, I felt the Lord tell me to drop all Transcendental Meditation practices, and I did."

Talking to Vail, one cannot help but sense that she has finally found the truth and fulfillment she had been looking for all her life.

A Berkeley Journalist Shares His Experience

Based in northern California, Brooks Alexander, thirty-eight, has a Master's degree in Political Science from a Texas university and has also spent three years in law school. Since 1969, he has been a free-lance researcher and writer, particularly in the area of the occult, Eastern religions, mysticism, and similar trips.

Brooks told me he had first learned about Transcendental Meditation techniques as early as 1965.

"I had been taking psychedelic drugs of various kinds for several years and was firmly committed to the search for that experience of unity and the vision of truth that opened up to me when I was 'high.' I moved into a hippie commune near Gerneyville, California. It seemed obvious to me there must be some simple technique of consciousness-alteration that bypassed drugs altogether. The classical spiritual disciplines of the East seemed to work, all right, but they were far from simple; they demanded a life-commitment and a life style that put them totally out of reach for the ordinary man in society. TM seemed to share the effectiveness of these techniques without having their limitations; it looked like my answer.

"I received my initiation in 1966, and very quickly discovered that TM does, in fact, deliver on its promise to affect certain features of one's inner experience. The Maharishi's technique of meditation does produce an alteration of consciousness, and it does get you high.

"Nevertheless, three years later, I stopped my meditation. Why? Because TM cannot deliver on the most important of all the promises it makes: the promise to produce a real solution to the human condition, the promise to produce a fundamental healing of the spiritual sickness of Man. The promise itself is clearly made. The Maharishi Mahesh Yogi plainly states that his technique of Yoga brings final fulfillment to all levels of human existence, that it can overcome the ultimate problems of despair, alienation and death. The Maharishi promises that through Transcendental Meditation one reaches a state of 'God-consciousness' in which 'action ceases to decay life . . . mental and physical planes come to the level of the spiritual plane which has eternal life.' *The Meditations of Maharishi Mahesh Yogi* (Bantam Books, p. 23).

"This is simply and obviously untrue. The plain fact is that death is the final enemy, not just of some men, but of all. No Sage or Yogi, however great, has ever failed to die. The Maharishi himself is visibly aging, and will also someday die. Indeed, the final failure of consciousness alteration and spiritual technology lies in the fact that it, too, is subject to the same law of decay and death that is responsible for our human condition—that ultimately *is* our human condition.

"No human achievement is eternal, just as no human being is immortal, no matter how 'conscious' he may be. Even as man boasts possession of the powers of a god, and lays claim in his consciousness to the title of 'God,' he remains, in brutal fact, a slave to the power of death.

"The reason that TM cannot truly deal with the fact of death is that it cannot truly deal with the fact of our alienation from God, which is the source of death. Indeed, the Maharishi teaches that there is only one reality in existence, which is God; that we are by nature a part of that Divine Reality, and only by ignorance or illusion do we falsely think ourselves cut off from it.

"The Maharishi's error is a common one. In meditation we transcend the forms of conceptual thought and experience the deep unity of our own being. Because Man is made in the image of God, it is easy to mistake this for an experience of God, or of union with God.

"I reached a point of spiritual crisis one night in October, 1969. Chanting the mantra 'Ram' (a Hindu god) just did not fill my spiritual vacuum. I found that there is one who does deal with death, and fully overcomes it. I stopped my meditation, because I met Jesus Christ. He is the one who does *not* err. His verdict on man is shockingly harsh, but His offer of pardon is free. He does not bring us techniques at all, but simply 'good news' of what He has done.

"Not only in His words, but in His deed and in His death, Jesus bluntly demonstrates that our separation from God is more than an ignorance of the mind, that it goes to the roots of our being: 'He was wounded for our transgressions, he was bruised for our iniquities: the

122

chastisement of our peace was upon him, and with his stripes we are healed' (Isa. 53:5 KJV). Those who can accept that offer of grace, ". . . He has now reconciled . . . in His fleshly body through death . . ." (Col. 1:22 NASB). That is His promise. In His resurrection, that promise is fulfilled. It is our visible validation that the death God died for us in Christ is the fountainhead of Life. That Life is offered freely to all."

CHAPTER XII

Two Yogis Get Really "Linked"

I first met Dr. Paul Sudhakar in 1967, in Calcutta, India. He was a frail man, about five feet ten inches tall, with attractive curly hair, and a warm smile. In fact, he really had a glowing spirit about him. I found myself one of a group of more than three hundred spellbound people with whom he shared the extraordinary story of his encounter with the ray of hope—Jesus Christ.

For twelve years Paul Sudhakar had been considered by many leaders, including the late Dr. Radha Krishnan, as one of India's finest Yogis. He was a Brahmin (highest caste priest) from South India, and a nephew of Ex-Defense Minister, Krishna Menon, and he had earned a doctorate degree at one of India's leading universities.

Dr. Sudhakar had a brilliant mind and was well schooled in religion. But being a Yogi at heart, he was in a search for truth and paths that would "link" or "unite" him to God. He had tried many teachers and religious practices to satisfy his quest.

One day someone suggested that he go and learn at the feet of the former President of India, Dr. Radha Krishnan, who was recognized as one of the world's greatest philosophers. So he went to Dr. Krishnan, and asked him to be his guru and to impart to him spiritual truth and enlightenment. At last, Dr. Sudhakar thought, he was finally going to be able to settle down and receive that for which he had been searching all his life.

124

To his utter surprise, Dr. Krishnan suggested to him that "the greatest guru" he could learn from is Jesus Christ. Dr. Sudhakar was taken aback and deeply disappointed at first. But deciding to heed the advice of his respected President, he set out to read the Bible, and investigate the claims of Jesus Christ.

It was not an easy road. The thought of conversion from Hinduism to Jesus Christ carried with it the possibilities of social ostracism and persecution. Then, too, the spiritual exposure to Christ and His teachings had its struggles, doubts and fears, because it became obvious that the power of Christ's truth, way and life would revolutionize his life.

The low point in Dr. Sudhakar's life came when, aside from being tormented by spiritual turmoil within, his body was covered with sores, and he was confined to a hospital bed. In his state of desperation, Paul told the captivated audience how he cried out to Jesus Christ. And Jesus Christ appeared to him in a vision. It was an electrifying moment. Christ was hanging on the cross of Calvary—bruised, blood-covered and partially skinned, almost as badly as a skinned animal hanging in a butcher's shop in one of India's meat markets.

In that instant, Paul Sudhakar realized the extent of Christ's sacrifice and how it could cleanse his own sin, heal his sick body, and make him a totally new person. He accepted the invitation of Jesus Christ: "follow Me!", and he received both spiritual salvation and physical healing. After this fantastic spiritual experience, he noticed the sores on his body were all gone.

After his encounter with the ray of hope, Jesus Christ, Paul Sudhakar resigned from his high government post, on the basis that he had received a higher calling. Today, he travels all over India, and to different parts of the world, to share his "new life" experience. He is now truly "linked" with Jesus Christ.

Another Yogi's Search Ends

The life search of Yogi Ishwar Dayal, my grandfather, came to a similar end. In 1896, at approximately twenty-eight years of age, "Nana" (Hindu word for grandfather) headed home to return from his wandering seclusion back to the mainstream of humanity. By now his hair was long, and his face was thickly bearded. The soles of his feet had hardened from much walking, his veins bulged from the effect of sustained stress. His heart was really no happier than when he left. But at least he felt he was six years farther down the road toward spiritual fulfillment.

Before returning to his home town of Laherai Sarai in the Darbhanga District of North Bihar State in India, he stopped at an open-air barber shop in a neighboring village. Under the shade of a tree, the place where village barbers traditionally practiced their trade close to the heart of nature, he had his hair cut and his beard shaved. Several pounds lighter than he had been six years before, he attired his tall, slim physical frame in the dhoti and kurta worn by the vast majority of males in India.

As he trekked back to Laherai Sarai, his mind was active with numerous questions. Was his wife alive? Would his relatives and friends recognize him? How would he relate to his son, now six years old?

One question was clearly answered when he arrived at the block of houses where all his relatives lived in "joint-family" style, a fairly prevalent social custom in

India: nobody recognized him. He identified himself to his relatives, lovingly embraced his six-year-old son, and asked if his wife was alive. She was, but according to the family custom, he was only allowed to see her at night. So he patiently waited until midnight before he could meet his wife, Anughra.

The next day there was an elaborate, joyous celebration which lasted for several days as friends and relatives joined together to welcome the wanderer home. He was not considered a "prodigal" by any means. He had not wandered away from God. Rather, he had gone on a quest to experience a "link" or "union" with God in the true Yogi spirit. He was even reinstated in his position as a trusted and valuable tax collector.

Much of the travel that was part of this job, he did on horseback, and one day, while riding through an open market place on a standard business trip, his attention was attracted to a large crowd of spectators. They were attentively gathered around a German missionary by the name of Miss Kate. Grandfather stopped, tied his horse at a nearby tree, and joined the crowd. The songs and the message presenting the gospel of Jesus Christ he heard were arresting. Never before had he encountered the truth about Jesus Christ and Christianity. He listened intently and thoughtfully, enchanted by its "newness." His curiosity got the better of him to the point that he decided at the end of the open-air meeting to buy, just for a few pennies, a Gospel of St. John (the fourth book in the New Testament), and take it home to read.

Undoubtedly, this was a risky decision. If any of his relatives ever found him reading non-Hindu religious literature they would surely destroy it. Which would be merely typical of Indian religious fanaticism.

Each time he read the Gospel of John in the ensuing weeks, he would go back to the German missionary lady, Miss Kate, with his questions. And being thoroughly schooled in religions, a Sanskrit scholar and an expositor of the Hindu scriptures, he had more than one point of reference for comparison.

Weeks of deliberating, questioning, honestly seeking and searching were concluded by a decision he expressed to Miss Kate. It was this: "I have decided I would like to accept Jesus Christ and Christianity!"

"Do you realize," asked Miss Kate, "that, because of your staunch Hindu background, you may have to give up something?"

"I am willing to give up anything to follow Jesus Christ," said Grandfather.

"The one thing you must not again give up is your wife and children," Miss Kate replied.

A family of relatives, a home in which he had partial ownership, a lucrative position in the Maharajah's court, a large piece of property, and his rich religious heritage—all these and more—suddenly had their value reduced in the estimation of my grandfather to nothing. The ray of hope had touched his life, and he was determined to follow Jesus Christ.

But, in such a hostile environment, it would be almost impossible. And so he cautiously planned their escape. He sent a message to his wife a few hours ahead of time through his son. He was going to take her out that night for a moonlit "Ganga Snan" meaning "river bath." Because of this, she was not to have on any jewelry or bring any valuables of any kind. The truth was, he was going to take her to a place where he could introduce her to Jesus Christ, the one who is able to administer

128

"spiritual baths" that cleanse us within. He did not want her to take any valuables, because he honestly believed he had found, in Jesus Christ, the most valuable treasure of all.

That night, the family escaped from the village never to return again. They traveled to the village where missionary Kate lived, and took up residence in a room she provided for them.

There followed a period of disciplining. The family took water baptism, following in the example of Jesus Christ who did so just before the start of His ministry. Many months were spent in Bible learning, discussion, study, and prayer. God used this as a time of deepening and preparation for my grandfather, for he later launched out into a full-time ministry of preaching and teaching and discipling others to Jesus Christ.

Life was by no means easy; the family had their share of problems even at this time. The death of a son caused by cholera had now only left one son and one daughter. Far more disheartening than that was the spiritual depression that it brought to my grandmother, Anughra Dayal. She even came to the point of suggesting the family return home and go back to their Hinduism. At this point, missionary Kate was a great source of strength, encouragement, and blessing to her. Through prayer and preserving faith in God, the problem was finally conquered.

Grandfather turned into a powerful disciple through fully conscious, prayerful Christian meditation. Each day began with prayer from 4:30 to 6:00, followed by breakfast, and then about two hours of reading out loud from the Bible. The remainder of the day was spent traveling from one village to another, telling others of the "good news" of the ray of hope. After becoming a Christian, he felt called to give up the smoking of "hashish" to which he had developed a heavy addiction. He literally threw the pipe away.

In 1911, another daughter was born to them, and in 1914 my mother, Gyanmani Dayal, was born. Between 1911 and 1914, he preached actively in the state of Uttar Pradesh, India, in Gazipur, and in Dalmianagur. In 1914 when World War I broke out, the German missionary, Miss Kate, had to leave. New American missionaries replaced her. One of them, the Rev. James Pickett, is now living in retirement in Columbus, Ohio.

On official retirement himself, Nana refused to accept any pension, saying "My Lord will provide." In reality, he never really retired from sharing the truth of Jesus Christ. Like his personal friend and colleague, the late Dr. E. Stanley Jones, Grandfather was infused with a dynamic spiritual zeal. Literally thousands responded to the truth of Jesus Christ, as he poured out his heart. And somewhere he found the time to write a book in Hindi, *Satya-Kiran*, meaning "The Ray of Hope," of which thousands of copies were sold.

Grandmother died in August, 1964. Forty days later Grandfather transcended to Heaven to meet his guru, Master and Lord, face to face. For a few days prior to his death, at the age of ninety-six, he was unable to speak or engage in most types of movement. He asked my mother to sing hymns of praise to the Lord Jesus Christ, and read scripture to him, especially the Book of Revelation. He would just smile and take it all in. He invoked God's blessing upon all around him in his own silent way, indicating to my mother that his final prayer was that she would be blessed with all spiritual blessings from God.

CHAPTER XIII

New Life Meditation

A Tale of Two Kingdoms

Have you ever been presented with a situation where the line of demarcation between the "imitation" and the "real" appears to be very fine? It's like an identical copy of an artist's original work. Unless you touch the copy and examine it closely and carefully, you cannot recognize the difference between the "imitation" and the "real." Satan, the enemy of God and mankind, has a way of counterfeiting spiritual truths and experiences which should never be mistaken for the genuine. Through a series of parables in the book of Matthew, Jesus Christ shared some vital truths about the Kingdom of God:

> 'The kingdom of Heaven is like treasure lying buried in a field. The man who found it, buried it again; and for sheer joy went and sold everything he had, and bought that field.

> 'Here is another picture of the kingdom of Heaven. A merchant looking out for fine pearls found one of very special value; so he went and sold everything he had, and bought it.

'Again the kingdom of Heaven is like a net let down into the sea, where fish of every kind were caught in it. When it was full, it was dragged ashore. Then the men sat down and collected the good fish into pails and threw the worthless away. That is how it will be at the end of time. The angels will go forth, and they will separate the wicked from the good, and throw them into the blazing furnace, the place of wailing and grinding of teeth.

'Have you understood all this?' he asked; and they answered, 'Yes.' He said to them, 'When, therefore, a teacher of the law has become a learner in the kingdom of Heaven, he is like a householder who can produce from his store both the new and the old.'

When He had finished these parables Jesus left that place, and came to His home town, where He taught the people in their synagogue (Matt. 13:44-53, NEB).

These are undoubtedly true; but, I would draw your attention to five of the basic truths that are expressed in the preceding passage:

1. *Seeking*—The Kingdom of God must be sought after. Jesus Christ said, "If you seek, you will find." Is there any difference between the seeking aspect of attentive Christian meditation, which finds its roots in the Kingdom of God, and the seeking aspect of transcendental and other forms of Eastern meditations which are rooted in the kingdom of the world and/or the Devil? Most certainly there is. TM seeks to "cope" with the old life patterns that are deviant. Christianity seeks to reinforce the new life patterns "with power from on high." TM seeks a tempo-

rary stop-gap measure. Christianity seeks permanent solutions to problems in and through Jesus Christ.

I was recently confronted with a young man named Sam, who had been a long time seeking for a religious experience in non-Christian religious and man-made doctrines. He said to me, "I've come to talk to you, because I've had it. I'm sick and tired of it all. Can you help me to know and experience the Lord Jesus Christ?" He was seeking the highest level of spiritual relationship available to mankind.

2. *Rejoicing*—The Kingdom of God brings great joy to the finder. The joy that TM claims to bring is, in fact, both partial and fleeting. It is partial because it is a by-product. The product is mind-induced anesthesia, and as a result you will experience some happiness at the temporary escape from reality. It will not permeate the fabric of your entire life. It is fleeting, because you have to keep coming back, over and over again, to the meditation seat. The joy that Christ offers through belief in Him is expressed in His words: "I came that your joy might 'remain' in you." The Christian can rejoice in complete and permanent joy, because Jesus Christ is centered in reality. It is more than just a spiritual high that fizzles out.

3. *Surrender*—TM will ask you for some time, money, effort, and self-discipline. But not for a total surrender of your whole and true "self." For this would demand repentance, conversion, and a change of life-style. But Jesus Christ does. He says, "Come follow me . . . ." This simply means saying, Lord, I give up; You take over! Those who seek the Kingdom of Jesus Christ must surrender all that they "have" and "are;" but the Lord may choose to return it to them many times over.

4. *Separation*—TM does not separate good and evil,

133

light and darkness. Because of its Hindu-based concept of a God that embraces both good and evil, and in order to maintain an appeal to "all," it is one of those "gray" spiritual experiences. Christianity is based on clean-cut decisions. In Christ's parable, the good and the bad fish were separated by His angels.

5. *Learning*—TM claims that it is possible to reach "perfection" or a perfect state. And even though the Maharishi claims this perfection, the claim does not ring true in an imperfect world of spiritually-fallen humans. It is based on a subjective, untested scale of values. Who can believe in and serve a God whose perfection is so easily obtainable? Christianity is based in the idea that we, after beginning the new life in Christ, are still "becoming" more like Him, as we yield to His enabling power. We are still learners—even though we be teachers. We are learning to become truly free. We are learning to become Christ-conscious rather than self-conscious. We are learning to become sensitive to God's plan for our lives. We are learning to be Christ-like in our loving. We are learning to become dependent on the power and leading of the Holy Spirit of God. We are learning to lead, by the quality of our life, more than by our words or our actions, others to Jesus Christ.

Rooted in an Unshakeable Kingdom and Unchangeable Person

The Judean Hills must have created an ideal atmosphere to elevate David, the song-writer and poet, to inspiring levels of meditation. So were the intensely religious and thought-provoking scenes of India for the late Dr. E. Stanley Jones. It has not, however, been the "outward situation" but rather the "inward attitude" that has made meditation a powerful experience. It is, in its essence, the spiritual vibrancy that comes with the "new life" attitudes and experience. This is the way of the Kingdom of God with its focal point in Jesus Christ. It is an unshakeable kingdom and unchanging person.

What It Is Not

"New-life," Christian meditation is not a mystical experience. There is nothing psychic or occult about it. Earlier in this book we referred to the Bible verses, Isaiah 45:18, 19, where God declared that He did not live in the realms of darkness or speak in secret. Jesus Christ is light and truth, with no deception or shady spiritual deals. Christian meditation is not another "kick," because it is more than bliss and demands purity of conscience.

Christian meditation is not impassive. It is filled with the divine energy and life of the Word and the presence of the Lord Himself. So sitting quietly in a corner with eyes shut will not and cannot be classified in the category of new-life meditation, if it is an impassive experience in Jesus Christ.

Christian meditation is not for the spiritually unprepared. There is no ritualistic initiation ceremony to bring one up to par, but rather the "linking" of Jesus Christ and the individual in a personal relationship. As Paul, the Apostle, exclaimed, the life of the Christian is ". . . hid with Christ in God" (Col. 3:3 KJV).

What Is Christian Meditation?

It is a decidedly Christ-centered experience, with the focus on Jesus Christ, His teachings and His presence. If you, as a Christian, are meditating on just any and everything, you are not involved in truly the highest form of new-life meditation.

The art of Christian meditation is progressively developed. It does not happen instantaneously, the moment we decide to follow Jesus Christ. In the Garden of Gethsemane, Christ found out that His disciples were not able to watch with Him in prayer and meditation for one hour. Their spirit was willing, but the flesh was still weak and needed discipline.

Christian meditation is active and need-fulfilling. "Active" does not necessarily mean "noisy." It refers to the spiritual energy of Jesus Christ flowing into and out of the individual meditator. The courage, strength, or miracle you may need, you can have by "faith-filled" focus on the person of Jesus Christ. Results follow prayerful, alert, and attentive meditation, for Christian meditation is directive. Jesus Christ confirmed this, when He said that the children of God are led by His Spirit. It is a natural, active process.

Is There Any Difference between Prayer and Meditation?

Technically, there really should not be. But, in our speedy generation, prayer of the "jiffy" variety is greatly lacking in meditative content. This is probably the major weakness you will find in the prayer life of Christian individuals. The way to "pray without ceasing" (I Thess. 5:17) is to cultivate a meditative state of mind. Christians can be even more powerful and fulfilled as individuals as they cultivate a meditative dimension to their prayer lives.

136

Who Can Experience It?

Christianity has sometimes been represented as being for a select few. But actual fact reveals that Jesus Christ came for all the world (John 3:16). Anybody who exercises faith and turns over his or her life to Christ, can experience the new life He offers and begin meditating on the highest level. Religion, caste, creed, color, and race are man-made distinctions. They cannot stand before the immeasurable magnitude of the depth and height of the love Jesus Christ has for all mankind. You do not need to improve yourself—that is God's business—you are received by *him* as a candidate, just because of your sincere desire.

If you have the desire and will to move into the stream of the new-life meditation, all you need to do is get yourself prepared by tuning in on the right wave-length.

How to Tune in on the Right Wave Length

1. Realize and visualize Jesus Christ—This is an "objective" step of weighing the issue. It entails a recognition of a sinful "self" and visualization of how Jesus Christ by His sacrifice on the Cross is able to meet your needs and make you a new person. What He promises, no one else can do. He can and will give you new life, if you really want it.

2. Turn around and look at Him—This is a "subjective" step. It requires more than an understanding of the issues involved; it requires a personal step of faith-filled commitment. This begins with a change of heart and mind toward your sinful "self" of the past, and is followed by a "catharsis" of confessing past misdeeds, and seeing Him, Jesus Christ, as the absolver and giver of new life, and your only way out of your present spiritual condition.

137

Just as Jesus Christ was resurrected from the dead into "newness of life," you can experience a spiritual resurrection in your own life—and start becoming like Jesus Christ. This is a totally new height of existence—dynamic, free, and contagious.

3. Actualize and receive Him—This is a "receptive" step. As you accept Jesus Christ and receive Him and His new-life experience, you become a true child of the God of the universe. You belong to His family. You become, in fact, a Christian Yogi. You are linked to the Lord and Creator of the universe. It is a personal link. It is a revolutionizing link. It is a permanent link.

The Focus

There is one and only one focus for the new-life Christian as he meditates. It is the person of Jesus Christ. As part of the triune God, He created the world (John 1:3). He is willing to be your Savior from sin and future judgment (John 3:16). You can imbibe His lordship in your life and be progressively conformed into His image. The hope in the promise of a glorious eternal future will become reality when He returns to the earth again (1 Thess. 4:16, 17).

The Frame of Reference?

A person without a value system or goal is a directionless person. The Bible is the frame of reference for Christian meditation. It is not based on mythology or intuitive theory, but is an inspired revelation of God, and its test is the practical, down-to-earth workability of its principles. There is nothing hazy or ambiguous about its central truth and nothing irrelevant about its nuts-and-bolts guidelines for living.

This is what makes it a fail-safe frame of reference. Our faith and belief in it puts the power and honor of Jesus Christ at stake—but you will find He always comes through for you! So before disputing or rejecting this frame of reference for meditation, why not honestly investigate it first. Pragmatically speaking, it will work!

How to Meditate Effectively

1. *Pull back from the rat race*—There is a difference between "pulling back" and "pulling out". Withdrawing from society into total seclusion is unhealthy and probably casts serious questions about the practicality of your spiritual faith. On the other hand, it is important to pull back (1) for an objective review of the situation. This is a mental action. (2) Relaxing yourself in a total way. This is physical. (3) Relinquishing or emptying out your mental distractions by committing them verbally to Jesus Christ. Nothing is hidden from Him anyhow. This is a spiritual act. This first step is the new-life perspective. You want your meditation to be solitary, relaxing, and relieving.

2. *Open up the channels*—Three basic obstacles seem to clog up the channels of communication between you and God and keep you from meditating effectively: (a) Self-enthrallment—this is overcome by praising and worship of the Lord Jesus Christ, the perfect Master. This point of comparison helps one to realize that one is not so great after all (Col. 2:10); (b) The next obstacle is sin, which is overcome by repentance and confession (1 John

139

1:9); and (c) Crying needs must be met—and God has promised to meet them (Phil. 4:19). Get these petitions out of your mind and into His hands.

3. *Intake*—Most often, we don't give God a chance to get a word in edgewise into our times of prayer and communication. The essence of meditation itself is right here at this level. Most of us end after the first two steps with an "Amen!" We have stopped short, quitting at the borderline of meditation.

Cease from talking to God—and establish a "listening post." This method has been especially endorsed by E. Stanley Jones over a period of at least sixty years as a Christian meditator. Allow God to speak to you. You will not, most often, hear any audible voice from heaven—though you may. You may just be impressed with a verse of scripture, a thought, a person in need.

Act as you feel led to do—as long as it is not in conflict with the God-given frame of reference, His Word, the Bible. God does not contradict Himself. There will be days when you may feel like you have received nothing. God may choose to speak to you through some other means (most often the lips of those around us), and we must not box Him in. This crucial stage is one of the new-life insights.

4. *Let it overflow*—You do not need to try to convert the world; God has given that assignment to the Holy Spirit (John 16:7–11). Your place in the world is to be His light—by letting it shine through your life. We are to share the message of new life as a natural life style. If we have to "crank up" our witness, as a general rule, we need to meditate longer and speak less. This is the new life "release." It's a bubbling-over experience. David, the

Psalmist, described it, saying, ". . . My cup runneth over" (Ps. 23:5 KJV). This is indicative of an unmechanical, uncalculated flow—at least as far as we are concerned. God knows what He is doing. Lack of "in-take" will limit the "overflow," and lack of "overflow," as we hold it in, will result in spiritual stagnation and staleness. Expression also deepens impression.

Cultivate a Meditative State of Mind

The scatter-gun approach is not as effective as the consistent, continual attitude of meditation. The meditative state of mind need not try over and over again merely to be able to cope with problems. Having experienced the new life, problems begin to work themselves out as the inflow of Christ's Spirit and truth overflow from the life of a meditative Christian. So it is an active, not passive, meditative pattern—active, not in the sense of being turbulent, but rather in the sense of being energetic.

When Joshua was assuming the reins of leadership from Moses in the Old Testament, God presented him with some positive guidelines to help him be the best leader he could possibly be. He was leading the Jews—who often turned out to be a "rough crowd." His responsibilities were weighty. The goal, to reach and dwell in the Promised Land, was certainly ambitious. The enemies around had to be contended with—foes that had to be overcome for the sake of Israel's safety and survival.

And there was Joshua's inexperience and youth. In the light of all these circumstances, God presented him with a set of guidelines for successful life and leadership which included a significant emphasis on meditation (Joshua

1:8). In fact, he was encouraged to meditate "day and night," or, in other words, to remain in a continual, meditative frame of mind and spirit.

Then there was the mature and experienced spiritual giant, the Apostle Paul. He had an intern, or associate evangelist, working with him by the name of Timothy. Timothy was open to learning and receiving valuable wisdom for the formative years of his youth and his ministry for his Lord. After outlining a series of duties in a letter to Timothy, Paul concludes by urging him to "meditate on these things"—and allow the Holy Spirit to further illuminate the truth contained in them, and work them deep into Timothy's heart.

The meditative state of mind begins to become a reality when, in the midst of the hustle and bustle of life, you don't feel spiritually stale, and instead are able to enjoy a fruitful communication with God, and allow Him to pour His thoughts, dreams, and visions into your mind and spirit. Life then takes on an indescribable dimension of excitement and fulfillment! You begin to realize that you are part of God's master plan, and your two-way communication unit is constantly alive with divine transmission.

No human being is free from periods of crisis. In fact, it sometimes seems like we move from crisis to crisis. But the crisis is actually sized up by one's ability to turn it over to God. The same problem could be for one person minor, for another, an insurmountable crisis. The meditative Christian with a focus on Jesus Christ, sizes up the situation from God's point of view instead of his own, which puts it in a much less formidable perspective, for in God, "all things are possible." He is motivated by a super-power that surges within his being and causes him to exclaim in his spirit, "I *can* do all things through Christ!"

The Christian meditator who is progressively practicing and developing the art of meditation will begin to experience continual streams of the peace of God (that peace which Christ said He would give, different from the kind the world has to offer), an inexpressible joy, powerful, creative insights, and an ever-increasing love for Jesus Christ and his fellow man.

The final result is an acid test. It is impossible to be a fulfilled Christian meditator, if you are loveless and cold-blooded. When you begin to imbibe the Spirit of Christ through meditation, love and compassion never cease to pour out of your life to others around you.

How Often Do I Meditate As a Christian?

The extent and the intent of Christian meditation varies from person to person. Some Christians may be struggling to say a prayer and meditate for ten minutes. Others can utilize ten minutes in a really meaningful meditative experience. So it seems hard to suggest a set amount of time. It does take time; Christian meditation is not meant to be a coping device alone, though this is one of its natural side benefits. It is aimed at making you the Christian you really want to be—the one that Christ wants you to be.

It does not matter how often you take time to meditate, it is never a waste of time. It may not always be a sensational occasion, but it is building up the inner spiritual person.

Some often ask how they can begin to become Christian meditators when they've never really done it before. Here are some steps to help you.

1. Ask God to help you—He wants you to meditate on

Jesus Christ and His Word; in fact, He's probably been waiting a long time for you to want to stop and really *listen* to Him.

2. Take advantage of times when you feel like being alone. These periods of time somehow find God-ward communication happening more easily—in spite of the fact that the first few minutes you may just be dozing or daydreaming. Begin to praise the Lord in the mind and spirit for different reasons that come to you.

3. Try to find a place where you can be undisturbed— some commuters even use the train—and form a habit of using the same place at the same time. Actually, you can meditate just about anywhere under almost any circumstances, but, as in anything new, it helps to have a target pattern.

4. If you are a high-geared individual, be sure to indulge in some form of physical relaxation each day, whatever physical exercise relaxes you. After you feel relaxed, you can begin to read the Bible imaginatively and ask God to speak to you. Or just still your mind, by acknowledging any nagging thoughts or concerns and giving them up to the Lord. Then ask Him to help you really concentrate and discipline your mind to stay attentive to the business at hand. Unfortunately, until we've had a good deal of practice, our mind is like a teen-age schoolchild, sitting in a classroom by an open window on a warm spring afternoon.

It is helpful to take Paul's advice (II Cor. 10:5) and bring all thoughts captive unto Christ, even though at first you may be shocked at how unruly your mind really is. But persevere—remember that Satan will be most anxious to discourage this venture into new depths of Christ, and will be running every possible distraction by your mind. Just

144

rebuke him, ask the Lord to cover your mind with His blood, don the helmet of salvation (in fact, the whole armor of God might not be a bad idea—see Eph. 6:13–18), and get back to the business at hand.

5. Be patient. And if nothing comes to you, be content to just quietly use the time to thank the Lord for all the blessings that come to mind. But *do* be patient, for one who has never practiced stillness of mind, silence—real silence—may be uncomfortable. Eventually, you will be able to hear God and converse with Him in a relaxed, easy fashion. Once a Christian begins to meditate, even if it is on a perfunctory level, and he tastes of it, he will begin to deeply desire to do more of it. Desire is always an important key.

Divine Guarantees—Sign Here!

The Holy Bible is filled with thousands of promises that are available to everyone who believes. If you are part of God's family through faith in Jesus Christ, these promises are for you. If you have not tried them out by "believing," you've been using the wrong methods. A check is only valid when you appropriate the money by signing your name. Don't expect God's promises to walk to you and begin to happen in your life and home—unless you sincerely believe with all your heart.

God has given us some fantastic promises for the Christian who meditates. An excellent summary of the primary spiritual benefits of Christian meditation are found in Joshua 1:8. Joshua was a winner, so they must have worked for him. They are: (1) the indwelling presence of the Word of truth in your life—as you meditate within this framework, (2) prosperity, (3) wisdom, and (4) success.

The benefits of meditation can literally revolutionize your life.

The entire world of humanity is in a never-ending search for guidelines and values. As you meditate within the frame of the principles of the Bible, you begin to receive guidance and a value system for your life. How do you use the Bible to meditate? Here are some ways: (1) Read, and then pray and meditate on what you read; (2) pray and ask God to assist your meditation when you read, saying "Lord, speak to me from Your Word; I'm ready to listen." You may read many verses, but only those that speak to your need will come alive to you.

Then there is the promise of "prosperity." This is not by any means limited to material things. It is a program of enrichment for your total being. So you will not miss out on being prosperous in spirit, in mind, in friends, and other areas of your life.

Wisdom is a benefit we could all use. But for the Christian meditator it becomes naturally available to him as he meditates. Many times one may not really know if he is acting in any special wisdom because God has just integrated it into your personality. But, if you carefully and thankfully examine your life, you will find it in there, threaded inseparably into your thoughts, speech, and action.

Success is on the way to the Christian meditator. This does not mean that he will never make mistakes. But it does mean that he will never have to be overwhelmed by a sense of failure—because God is able to work out everything for good, in spite of what we may do. A failure complex can result in depression, inferiority complexes, unhealthy social withdrawal, and in extreme cases, even suicide. But in Christian meditation, you will never have to be a victim of that type of negative results. You will be a success—by God's grace and with His help!

After years of research and personal experience, no form of meditation that I have tested has been able to make promises like we have just presented, and then actually come up with the goods. This is what makes the Bible and Christ-centered meditation almost "too good to be true." But it is available and open to all.

Keep Moving On . . .

Time marches on, sometimes imperceptibly, but nevertheless, very surely. The great search for truth seems unending and every generation seems to be in a state of spiritual upheaval and transition. If you are "moving" in your search for truth and total fulfillment in life with an open, seeking heart and mind—you will find. Every generation has its searching masses, and every generation has its finders—people for whom the search has ended.

The meditators will come and go—but the ray of hope shines on forever. Yesterday the West rose in the East. Today East rises in the West. But yesterday, today and tomorrow, Jesus Christ, "The Ray of Hope," pierces through to the consciousness of all humanity—shedding Light and imparting Life to all who believe.

* * *

Please address correspondence to the author at the following address:

PO Box 2442, Dublin, California 94566

For a free copy of

LOGOS JOURNAL

send your name and address to

Logos Journal

Box 191

Plainfield, New Jersey 07060

and say, "one free Journal, please."